Please Laugh With Me

Humorous Poetry

&

Poetry About
Love And Life

Please Laugh With Me

Humorous Poetry

&

Poetry About
Love And Life

by

Thomas Ian Graham

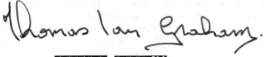

AVON BOOKS
1 DOVEDALE STUDIOS
465 BATTERSEA PARK ROAD
LONDON SW11 4LR

Printed and bound in the U.K.

Avon Books

London
First Published 1998
© Thomas Ian Graham 1998
ISBN 1 86033 826 7

CONTENTS
PART ONE: PLEASE LAUGH WITH ME

PART TWO: POETRY ABOUT LOVE AND LIFE

PART I

PLEASE
LAUGH WITH ME

Humorous Poetry

Please laugh with me
And share in my fun,
Inside this book
You will discover the sun!

On each page you'll find
Nothing dirty or lewd,
It's just full of laughs
And not awfully rude!

Now pull up a chair
And cast away that frown,
Please join with me in laughter
I'm the one who's the clown!

BEEF IS NOT ON THE MENU

We are having fish and chips tomorrow,
That's a meal that is really great!
With a couple of pickled onions
And mushy peas on a plate!

I used to like a nice big steak
But now it's not the same,
Some folks' brains have turned to sponge
And the cows have gone insane!

I have tried a curry now and then
But it's never been too hot,
Mind, I'm not a great lover of spicy food
It tends to drive me on the pot!

I tried an Indian only the once,
They called it a Vindaloo!
By gum that certainly made me shift
And it made my bum hot too!

Now I'm not a great lover of pasta
And a pizza soon fills up my tum,
I can't say it does really anything for me
Apart from it doesn't make me run!

Frogs' legs, well, I just haven't got a taste for,
I don't think they look all that kop!
Mind, they do say French cuisine is exceptional
But it might just put me on the hop!

I have to admit to being a fish and chip lover,
It is something that our table will grace,
I still think of roast beef and Yorkshire pudding,
But now beef is the one in disgrace!

THE STICKY BUN

It was early morning on my wedding day
And I was just feeling so great!
I had arisen quite early for the state I was in
And to say I was out pretty late!

The whole house was really buzzing
And everyone was running around!
There's a queue outside the bathroom
And there's no soap, someone has found!

Now the telephone has started ringing
"Will someone please answer that?"
It was mother's voice that I was hearing
Making breakfast from in the back!

It was the florist, they quickly informed me,
The buttonholes were now ready!
Mind, the way that my poor legs were acting
I wasn't feeling all that steady!

"What do you want for your breakfast?"
My mother was calling out again.
"I'll have a sticky bun, with some jam on!" I cried.
"Alright!" she said, "But you are a pain!!"

Well, now the time was really flying
And mother was in a bit of a gloom,
So I picked up my bun and I left her
And took it upstairs into my room!

Now I put my shirt and my tie on
And then I fastened up my trousers with my belt,
But when I came to eat my sticky bun up
It was suddenly quite missing, I felt!!

Well, I looked all over the bedroom
Under the bed and on top of the chair!
And at the end of all my searching
I found my bun just was not there!!

I thought that someone was playing a prank
So I got dressed, and I was ready to go,
But then when I looked at my watch
I realised it was ten minutes slow!!

And then came a shout from the landing,
The cars were suddenly here!
So I quickly made my way to the hallway
And everyone gave out a great cheer!!

Now, I was stood in the church with my best man
And the organ started up *Here comes the Bride!*
Then in even less than a few minutes
My bride was stood by my side!

My best man put the ring on the bible,
My hand was clammy, so I brushed it against the side of my bum!
And then what do you think I discovered?
Yes! It was my elusive squashed sticky bun!!

I'M NO COOK!

I'm not all that good at cooking,
Maybe I have never really tried,
I find boiling potatoes quite easy,
Or chips, if you like them fried.

I used to experiment in the kitchen,
But nothing ever turned out as it should,
I tried baking a potato in its jacket
And ended up with a half-baked spud.

I was given a recipe for a sauce mix
And in the pan it looked creamy and wet,
But when it was poured over the dinner
The darned sauce curdled and set.

Now you can't please everyone sat at the table,
But we all try to do our level best.
Someone said that they didn't like rabbit!
So I told them it was chicken breast.

Now I can make a pretty good omelette
And toss it like a pancake through the air!
Unfortunately I'm not the very best of catchers
And sometimes my pan isn't quite there.

I've tried my hand at making a curry
And thrown most everything into the pot,
But when I've sat down to my dinner
I found I'd made it too blooming hot.

The worst thing for me in the kitchen
Is to study the recipe book,
Because after I've finished my creation
It tells me I can't flipping well cook!!

MASH

I've got what it takes to be a couch bum!
But my missus has other ideas -
As soon as she sees me put my feet up
She gives me a flea in both my ears!

Now it's not that I'm lazy or anything,
Mind, I put in some practice when I can.
But there's times when I don't hear her coming
And she lands me, with one hell of a bang!!

Now, I've got the right build for a couch potato,
I'm kind of rounded in all the wrong places,
I've a face like a crisp packet that's been sat on,
And when I'm slonking, I have no airs or graces.

It's great to get in front of the telly
And let your belly just hang within sight,
Like a hippo that's appeared out of the water
And it suddenly gives everyone a fright!!

The remote control is the greatest invention,
I don't have to exert myself at all,
And when we get a thousand more channels
Then I'm really going to have myself a ball!

Now I've never been much of a smoker
Because when you're drinking, the fag gets in the way,
So I'm more of a couch slouching drinker,
And when the wife's out, that's the height of my day!

But there's nowt worse than when I've just gotten settled,
I'm in repose, and I've just topped up my glass,
When suddenly I see her face at the window -
And this couch potato suddenly becomes Mash!!

BARBECUED LUNCH!

We were visiting some friends not long ago
And it was a lovely sunny day,
The kids were all outside playing
And we were just chatting away.

They asked us if we would like to stay for lunch
As they were having a barbecue?
Now my wife and I both like eating outside
So we said that we'd share in their do!

Now my friend began mixing some punch
And he said, "I won't be making it too strong!"
Then I picked up a bottle, smelled it and said,
"My word! This doesn't half pong!!"

"The father-in-law brought it round!" he said,
"And he told me to add it to the punch,
It isn't very strong!" he mentioned,
"And it will go very well with our lunch."

So he went and poured in the bottle
And then we helped ourselves to a steak.
In walked my friend's father-in-law smiling,
He said, "I'll have some of that punch, it looks great!"

Now people were starteing to stagger about,
I said, "By heck! That's darned good stuff!
What was in that bottle you left?" I asked him.
"I didn't!" he replied, "It wasn't good enough!!"

Then one of the kids started crying,
He couldn't find the fuel for his model plane.
Suddenly there was an almighty flash
And someone screamed out in pain!!

The alcohol fuel for the model plane
Had been mixed well into the punch,
And someone with a touch of wind
Had put paid to our barbecued lunch!!

6

RABBITS

Now I love all kinds of animals
But of rabbits I am particularly fond!
I like watching their antics, as they bob up and down,
And then quickly vanish beneath the ground!

People say they are very destructive!
But all animals have a down side to their nature.
Rabbits will chew almost anything around
And digging up the ground to them's an adventure!

It's just lovely to watch the baby rabbits,
They look just like bundles of fur,
But there's a lot of predators running around,
So the big ones watch over them with care!

There's a lot of folk take rabbits for pets,
But personally I don't think that is right!
Animals are not meant to be put into cages
And anyway, sometimes the darned things bite!!

Now the people who breed them for showing
Like competition and hold a great sense of pride,
And I suppose they are conserving the animal,
Even though it isn't outside!

I must admit that I've seen all kinds of rabbits.
There's certainly a good variety about
And some of them are almost as big as children,
But their ears tend to make them stand out!

Yes, I have always had a fondness for rabbits
They're the animal that's always caught my eye!
Especially it they are wrapped up in a nice thick crust,
Because there's nothing nicer than rabbit pie!!

BLACK BEAN SOUP

Dedicated to Barrows Wild West Rangers,
in particular to Mr. Ron Newton and his wife Nancy.

I was ridin' on a railroad train
dressed up in my cowboy gear,
I was really havin' a darned good time
Swillin' down lots of beer.

The women there were pretty frisky
And them nights sure got mighty hot!!
Mind, I weren't told about the fellas,
They sure are a pretty good shot!!

Now I was chatting up a real nice gal
And swiggin' down a bottle of beer
When suddenly a low-down cowpoke
Shot off a piece of my ear!!

"Hey!" I yelled, "Look at what you've done!
Now that's no way to treat a friend!!"
He replied, "If'n you hadn't of been smilin'
I'd of blown off yer rear end!!"

The gal let out a holler and cried,
"Please don't hurt him anymore!
I've got the hots for this smooth-talkin' Englishman
And I'm takin' him home to meet Pa."

The cowpoke rubbed his grizzly chin
And said, "You'd better make it mighty quick!!
Before I blow his head off
And separate him from his wick!!"

The gal pulled the communication cord
And I let out a rebel cry!!
I thought I was goin' to meet my maker,
My time had surely come to die!!

We scrambled along the railroad track
Until we saw a broken down old cabin.
The gal yelled out, "Hey, Pa! It's me!
And I'm totin' my belovin'!"

Now this old coot emerged from the shack
And he was carryin' a buffalo gun!!
"So you're gonna get wed?" he smiled at me
And aimed it away from my bum!!

I threw my hands up in protest!
I just wanted to voice my concern.
He said, "It won't cost you a penny, son,
Unless you have money to burn!"

Then along came the day of the weddin'
And up sidled the preacher called Jake.
But then in the middle of the ceremony
I asked, "Where's the weddin' cake??"

Suddenly my bride started agrinnin'
And she let out a loud cock-a-hoop!
She said, "We ain't havin' weddin' cake, darlin',
We're havin' Ma's home-made black bean soup!!"

THE IRON FRYING PAN

My husband's gone and left me, he didn't say goodbye,
Mind, I really don't miss him at all,
He was one of the laziest bums you'd ever chance to meet
And he wouldn't work! All he wanted was the dole.

He would never take a bath, and always had an awful smell,
Like being down wind to a pig farm or manure.
When the water shortage came about, it was then he liked to flout
His hairy chest, and odour lacking demure.

He never changed his clothes, they were dirty and full of holes,
And his socks were in a sad state of repair,
His feet were always smelly, and he had a beer belly,
And he never bothered to even comb his hair.

He had tattoos that were obscene, in places best not seen,
And his teeth were simply dropping out of his head.
His breath had an awful smell, like something rotting in a well,
And if it caught you, it made you think of something dead.

He was as deaf as a post, and would never hear a holocaust,
Nothing would ever move him off his ass,
And if a bomb should go off, he'd just clear his throat and cough,
Then he would fill himself up another glass.

His language was terrible, and his looks were quite obscene,
I don't know why I took to him at all,
His legs were pretty bandy, and he always looked cross-eyed,
And when he spoke, all he ever did was bawl.

Well, now he's gone and left me, I feel better in myself,
And I'm sure he feels a much better man,
I don't think the fall killed him, when I pushed him down the stairs,
I think it was the blow from the iron frying pan!!

SANDWICHES FOR LUNCH?

I used to work in the shipyard,
And lots of things changed through the years,
Particularly the tales that the lads used to tell,
Sometimes they really had me in tears.

Years ago, well before my time,
They used to have a communal loo
That meant you didn't sit in cubicles,
Everyone sat together in view!

Well, it meant that you never felt lonely
And you could pass the newspaper along,
And if any of you felt like humming a tune
Then you could all join in with a song.

Sometimes, it was the only chance for a natter,
Because the bosses were strict on the time!
And they always made sure about their pound of flesh,
Making sure everyone toed the line!

Now, they used to hang their coats behind them
And one day a coat fell into the loo.
Well, the workman rolled up his sleeves and said,
"Oh dear, what a to-do!!"

And then he felt around in the toilet
And brought his jacket back out of the pan!
All of the lads looked on disgusted
And said, "You can't wear that again Sam!"

"I'm not wearing this again!" he said smiling,
"Anyway, it's got nowt to do with you bunch!!"
Then he put his hand in the jacket pocket
And took out the sandwiches for his lunch!!

OUT TO LUNCH

It's blowing a gale, boy, it isn't half cold,
It has just blown my hat off, I'm glad I'm not bald!
The weather is freezing, now I'm going to sneeze,
I sure felt the vibration, right down to my knees.

My fingers are blue, and my toes are like ice,
When I looked out the window, the day seemed quite nice.
But now I'm out walking, here in the flippin' cold,
And I'm not feeling so brave or bloomin' bold!

My head's frozen over. My hair's gone quite stiff,
But if I was to comb it, I wouldn't get a quiff,
I have water in my ears, and icicles under my nose,
And what's up with my feet? I can't feel my toes.

My ears are tingling with the cold icy blast,
Now my nose has started to run, I don't think I'm going to last.
I am all frozen over, from my head to my toes,
Now there's sleet coming down. I'm all wet as well as froze!

My bloomin' coat's blown wide open, and my button's come off,
My throat's getting sore, and it's making me cough,
The water's seeped in, to every crevice that I've got,
And the way that I feel, I think that I've had my lot!

I've battled on through the wind, the rain and the snow,
I feel like an intrepid hero, who's putting on a show!
Now I've grabbed hold of a corner, to pull myself round,
But another icy blast just spins me to the ground.

I fought back to round the corner, now my objective's in sight,
And then I struggled across the road, that took some might.
I scrambled to the doorway, and then came the crunch -
There's a note on the door saying, "Sorry, gone out to lunch"!!

A CUP OF TEA IS AWFULLY NICE!

They say that we're a nation of tea drinkers,
Well, I reckon that is rightly so,
Because when I am visiting people
The teapot's always on the go!

"Excuse me, do you take milk and sugar?
Now be careful it isn't too hot.
Would you like a cup and saucer?
Or a mug with your name on the pot!"

"Are you a person who uses tea bags?
Or holds a strainer over the cup instead?
Would you prefer your tea at the table?
Or maybe you'd like it in bed!!"

Some people take tea made with lemon,
While others prefer it with ice,
I like having a good chat over a cuppa
I don't think there's anything as nice!

It's lovely to have tea and biscuits
With friends who have dropped in for a chat,
There's nothing like a little bit of gossip
Or ten minutes of chewing the fat!!

Whether we sit around looking quite formal
Or we are relaxed, in an informal way,
Then I reckon that this nation of tea drinkers
Will never let the teapot go astray.

So I say to the yanks, "Keep your coffee!!"
And to the chinese, "You can lock away your spice!"
Because for me, when the kettle is boiling,
I find a hot cup of tea awfully nice!!

I'M NOT A BIG DRINKING MAN!

Now I'm not a big drinking man!
But I do like to enjoy a drink
Not enough to make me legless,
Or too much so's I can't think!

There's nowt wrong with being sociable,
It's lovely to share in a tipple,
Just as long as you don't go overboard
And your legs begin to wobble!

I very rarely drink from cans,
I much sooner prefer a glass,
Well, I like to see what I'm drinking,
And I'm in a far better class!

Some folks will sup from sweaty clogs,
While others sip from slippers,
But I'm a man who would like to think
That I've never acted so flippant.

I was invited to a cheese and wine do:
A store was holding a promotion,
But after I'd finished supping the wine
I got thrown out in a commotion!!

I've never been a Champagne Charlie,
I sooner prefer Newcastle Brown!
I've never swilled it around my mouth,
I just like to get it down!!

A lot of men can hold their drink
While others just want to fight!
Me, well, I like to enjoy myself
Then get my head down for the night!!

CELEBRATED ON THE HOUR

I was passing by a pub one night, my heart was feeling light,
When suddenly a door flew open, and gave me such a fright.
This fella came flying out, and knocked me over to the ground,
He looked at me and said, "Sorry! C'mon, let me buy you a round."

He picked me up and dragged me in, and sat me at a table.
I protested! "Now," he stated, "I'm celebrating while I'm able."
He was a big man with a kindly face, I wouldn't spoil his cheer,
'OK!" I said, and made it known, that I'd have a pint of beer.

When he sat beside me, I could tell he was the worst for wear.
"What's the celebration?" I asked, as I stopped him sliding off his chair.
"My wife has gone and left me!" he laughed. "And I'm now a happy man.
Trouble is, she's taken everything I own, and left me in a jam.

"But what the hell, time will tell that she's not as happy as me,
Because I've stopped all the payments, so she's gotten nothing free.
She was an awful woman, and treated me less than a dog,
One day she smacked me in the kisser, all I wanted was a snog.

"Her cooking was diabolical, and her clothes! She always looked a mess.
She had no pride, and she took all my money, leaving me penniless.
There wasn't a mirror in the house, she'd taken them all down,
She had the funniest face you've ever seen, even funnier than a clown."

"What made you marry her?" I asked. "Well, I loved her!" he said, frowning.
"Mind, I hadn't seen her stripped! Then I thought, she'd look better in embalming.
She didn't have a bust!" he said. "In fact, she had no figure there.
I've seen more shape in our old couch, and more meat on the easy chair!"

He swallowed down his pint of brown, then choked and turned a funny colour.
He grabbed his whisky, and knocked it back before sliding to the floor.
The barman approached, looked down and said, "Well, this time it's all over.
His wife left him over thirty years ago, he always celebrated on the hour!"

15

ALL FOR THE WANT OF A NAIL!

I'd decided on some renovating
And add an extension to the house,
Some doors were pretty ill-fitting,
And in one room, you couldn't swing a mouse!

I dug foundations in the garden,
Then my wife said, "Don't forget the heating!"
I chased out a channel for the pipework,
The gas fire it would be feeding!

I put up walls and laid the floor,
Then the pipe started sagging,
So I got some wood to block it up
But a nail I found was missing!

I came upon some rotten old string
And fastened it to the pipe,
There, that will do for now! I thought,
Later on I'll put it right!

I carried on with the job in hand,
Three months later all was finished.
Everyone came to admire my work
Just to see what I'd accomplished.

We sent our heaps of invitations
Well, we had decided to celebrate!
I turned on the Central Heating
And lit the gas fire in the grate!

Loads of people turned up for the party,
Suddenly there was a rumbling sound,
It came from beneath the floorboards
Then everything blew up around!!

The walls fell out onto the garden,
Most of the ceiling fell onto my head,
I took a quick look at the gathering
But couldn't see anyone dead!!

16

My wife had been visiting the bathroom
And suddenly found herself in the hall,
An irate neighbour had come round complaining,
When she landed, he broke her fall!!

The gas moved along the main sewer
And blew up ten houses in the street,
A guest who had previously been boasting
Saw his bungalow end up in a heap!!

The mayor just happened to be passing
In his Rolls Royce all shiny and new,
When a tree, uprooted by the pressure,
Squashed it, and the mayor turned the air blue!!

The fire brigade arrived with the constabulary,
And the kindly police let me out on bail,
I just couldn't believe all the carnage
And all for the want of a N.A.I.L.

WALL-PAPERING'S A REAL PAIN!

Wall-papering is a real pain!
And having to pick out the pattern,
Will that do? or is that the one?
Maybe, perhaps or 'appen!

How many rolls will we have to use?
Will it have to be matched up?
Should I add the paste from the packet?
Or perhaps mix it by the cup?

Now I've made the paste too watery
And it's running down the wall!
Oh dear, the paper keeps on falling off!
It just won't stick at all!!

Can you tell if the pattern's right way up?
Or do you think it's upside down?
Now, is that the pattern that we chose?
Because it's beginning to get me down!!

I tried to shape it around a corner
But it drove me around the bend!
And then when I thought that I'd finished
I couldn't find the bloomin' end!!

And then while coming down the ladder
I suddenly slipped on some wet paste!
And I ripped the paper off the wall,
My panic had caused the waste!

My wife said, "C'mon and have a cup of tea!
And then we'll show it who's the master.
If we both get stuck in together
It will get done a whole lot faster!"

I spilled some bloomin' tea on the paper
And in my haste I grabbed a wet cloth,
But when I wiped the paper over
I found I'd cleaned most of the pattern off!

18

I muttered to her, "I didn't like this paper!!
But you had to have your way!
We've gone and bought a lot of rubbish
And now it's turning a funny grey!!"

My wife broke down in tears and said,
"I thought we would save some money!
We should have bought the vinyl
But it was going to cost a lot more money!!"

Now when we had finally finished the papering
It didn't look at all too bad!
It was only when we put the light on
That the paper looked awfully sad!!

No, I'm not a one for papering,
I'm always glad when the last piece is on.
I'd like to think that's the last piece I'll stick,
Someone else can do it when I'm dead and gone!!

D.I.Y.

Whoever it was that first thought about D.I.Y,
They want to come back and finish it off!
Because when I'm doing improvements to my old house
Something usually decides to drop off!!

If I decide to do a little bit of plumbing
Because a leak has decided to spout,
I like to repair it as fast as I can
Before mushrooms begin to sprout!!

Now I'm not very good at bricklaying,
But like most things, I've given it my best.
I built a small wall, but the wind blew it down,
I guess it just wanted a rest!

It's amazing what you find under floorboards,
I found a cat that was making a din!
And after I'd discovered the error
I knew it was me who had fastened it in!!

Now gas is something that I won't tamper with
Because you never know when it's going to ignite!
I know a fella who blew half his house up
Because he decided to strike a light!!

Electricity, now that can cause problems!
Especially if you are working in the dark.
There's always someone wanting to plug something in
And make you light up just like a bright spark!!

I have had a really good go at roofing,
And that certainly put me to the test!
It was winter, and frost had descended white on the ground,
But the way that I came down wasn't the best!!

I bought a paraffin lamp to do some paint stripping
And the paint came away like a shot!
But I couldn't touch anything for days on end
Because everything got too bloomin' hot!!

I had decided to install some windows
And I measured them out in the rain!
But when I came to fit in the glass
It just went straight through the bloomin' frame!!

I had a salesman call round the other day,
He stuttered and said, "Look at the money you're savin'!"
I thought I'd bought a carpet to cover the floor
But instead I got some crazy pavin'!!

Now you have to watch these house-callers,
Because they're just fly boys in the know.
A friend of mine bought a lovely lawn,
He's just waiting for the seeds to grow!!

D.I.Y. can be a whole lot of trouble,
Especially if you aren't that way inclined,
So if after you've done, and some people make fun,
Just give them a good kick up their behind!!

IT ALWAYS RAINS WHEN I'M UP A LADDER!

Why is it when I'm working up a ladder
That it will always decide to rain?
And when I have rushed to get out of the weather
The sun shows his smiling face again!!

I'll wait and wait for the weather to become settled
And then finally, on that fateful day,
I have run around getting everything ready,
Maybe I should have decided to pray!!

I find that my ladders won't reach where I want them,
There is nothing worse than a ballerina on high!
Standing on one leg, pirouetting with a paint brush,
Making gestures, as though trying to paint the sky!

And then the heavens decide it's time to open!
Now let's see what's on offer today?
I could give you a little sun and lots of showers,
Or a gale that will simply blow you away!!

And maybe perhaps a crackle or two of thunder?
With a flash of lightning, to make things more bright!
I have been known to throw in a few hailstones
But I don't want you to snuff it through fright!!

Now thunder and lightning always looks spectacular,
Especially when you are high up off the ground,
But if it strikes awfully close to where I'm working
Then I have had to change my underpants, I've found!!

Now I don't mind rain too much, when it's only drizzle.
But it is overmuch, when it's running down my neck,
Especially if what I'm brushing on is emulsion
And it's running down my walls just like a beck!!

TRIAL AND ERROR

My brother-in-law's a bit of a disaster,
He painted his ceiling and door,
But when he walked in from the kitchen
He forgot that he'd painted the floor!

He found that he had some left over,
So then he made the bathroom look neat,
But when he sat down on the toilet
He forgot that he'd painted the seat!

This man is quite unbelievable,
But I believe he's started a new trend.
When he dropped his watch down the loo pan
It stopped before going round the bend!

Then he fished it out with a bit of bent wire
And shouted, "It's okay, it's waterproof!"
But when he saw his wrist turning emerald green
Then he practically went through the roof!

He enlisted in the Territorial Army
And they issued him with a camouflage suit.
But whilst answering the call of nature
He got stung by a horny-tailed brute!

He flew through the terrain in a fervour,
He felt that he'd never been so confused,
And when he finally got back to the roadside
His backside was all black and bruised.

When he reached camp he knocked up a curry
But he made the food too bloomin' hot,
And when the lads caught sight of him running
They thought he'd been bloody well shot!!

I'M NOT MAN OF THESE TIMES

I don't like the modern world, I belong to the past,
For whatever you go and buy these days isn't built to last.
I've put together a coffee table, wardrobes, and sink-units in a pack
And when I've finished their assembly, I have had to take them back

Bits of them are missing, and other parts don't fit,
I'm walking back and forward, like a bloody silly nit,
My wife asks, "Is it finished? You said you'd have it done today!"
I retort, "The damn thing fell apart, now it's back in the shop to stay."

I bought some paint a while ago, it said "non-drip dry" on the label.
I painted the chairs, it didn't drip, and it didn't dry! Now we stand around the table.
These hi-fi's and computers, their instructions are hard to beat,
I installed a system, now you can hear Elvis when you lift the lavatory seat.

A fella I know put a cupboard up, and it really did stand tall,
The cupboard fell down, he wasn't dismayed, its back is still attached to the wall.
He decided to put some shelves up, but to drill he had to lay on his belly.
He forgot he was working with plaster board, now he can watch next door's telly.

A man I know, bought himself some wood, to make some window frames,
And a neighbour, who was jealous, kept calling him awful names.
The man turned around with his rule in his hand, and said, "Don't you be so smutty!
When you put your windows in, all the glass fell out, because
You couldn't tell s**t from putty!"

24

THE SHADOW

This room's become decidedly tardy,
A surprise statement made by my wife,
"Yes, it's due for a face-lift!" she added,
It'll only take a few days out of your life."

I began to strip off the old wall-paper
And burnt off and sandpapered the old paint,
I filled in one or two holes in the plaster
And began to feel like a saint.

The room started coming together,
I applied paint to the skirting and doors,
New wallpaper brightened the room up
And I laid a new carpet on the floor.

Then a stain mysteriously appeared in a corner,
My wife scrubbed and scrubbed at the spot,
But no matter how hard she scrubbed it
She couldn't get rid of the blot.

I called in a professional decorator,
He applied a solution to the spot,
But when the decorator had left us
Back came the mysterious blot.

I called in a reputable builder,
He knocked all the plaster off the wall,
And after he'd finished skimming it over
We couldn't see the stain at all.

I arose quite early in the morning
And once again the stain had appeared,
I pushed the television out of the way
And suddenly the stain disappeared!

BARGAINS

I'm quite a one for the bargains, I like to think that I'm cutting the cost,
But each time I buy a money-saver, I'm always the one who's lost.
They say you learn the hard way, but I never learn the sense,
Each time I've saved a few more bob, it's cost me more in pence.

I bought myself a wristwatch, for a price too good to miss,
The man who took my money said it was a genuine Rolex Swiss.
I wore it at a party, and showed it off with pride
But then it fell to pieces, and had no works inside.

I bought a tea set from the market, it was marked down in price,
The plates had a lovely pattern, and the cups were wrapped up nice.
Then one evening we had visitors, and I decided to get it out,
I found the cups had no handles, and the teapot had no spout.

Now I don't buy jigsaws as a rule, because I don't find them exciting,
But I bought one a while ago, because I thought it was a saving.
It said "Over three thousand pieces," and was a picture of children
skipping,
But when I came to fit the final piece, I found that it was missing.

I bought my wife a Hoover, from a car boot sale last week,
He said he wanted twenty pounds, I said, "What a bloomin' cheek!"
I took it home and plugged it in, it made such an awful racket,
Then suddenly it blew up and wrecked the room, that cost me a packet.

I bought a first edition, because I thought it rather cheap,
It was all about a murder, and the plot was really deep.
I wanted to reach the end of the story, and find how it came about,
But when I reached the final chapter, the last page had been ripped out!!

I bought a toaster in a half price sale, I thought it was a snip,
But when I tried to take the toast out, it wouldn't relax it's grip.
I hit it with a hammer, and belted it with a brick,
And when it coughed my bread back, it sure looked mighty sick.

I ONCE LIVED IN THE CITY

I once lived in the city, it's a very busy place,
Everything's hustle and bustle, and everyone's in a race.
There's plenty of variety, for things to do and see,
With markets by the dozen, but nothing's going free.

There's wide boys in the city, after all that they can get,
Looking for the town folk, who they know are pretty wet,
They suck them in like a Hoover, then drop them when they're skint,
You're no good to them anymore, when they find out your pink lint.

They flog towels on the market, with colours that are nice to see,
And if you buy half a dozen, they chuck in a couple more free.
Mind; you're not supposed to use them, just hang them over the bath,
I know of a fella that used one, and he broke out in a rash.

A woman I knew put her hand up, and bought rolls of toilet paper,
I think she wanted something for the wall, but the price came pretty near.
And when she visited the toilet, she found she was constipated
Then yards and yards came off the roll, because it wasn't perforated.

A bloke I know bought a hosepipe, he got it for a good price,
And when he turned the tap on, he said, "My, that's awfully nice!"
He was holding the end of the hose, waiting for the water to appear,
But his place had turned into Kew Gardens, when a hundred holes appeared.

I bought a fancy toilet brush, it looked pretty good for the cash,
I was told the bristles were real hair, and the handle was made of brass.
But when my wife cleaned the toilet, its head fell down the pan,
And then I had to call for a plumber, to get us out of the jam.

Ticket touts are favourite, they want to get hold of your dough,
They'll flog you a couple of tickets, to get you into the back row.
But when you turn up early, and the seats are already took,
It's then you wish you were someplace else, curled up with a book.

FISHING!

I thought that I would try a spot of fishing.
It took me ages to put a worm on my hook!
But then I was told that if I caught any fishes
Then it would have to be a really big flook!!

Well, pretty soon I'd got myself into the river
But the fish hid, because they thought it was a game!
And then when I thought that I had caught a Big One
I reeled in a sink and bicycle frame!!

I spotted a boy with some string and a bent pin,
I laughed and called out to my wife,
Suddenly he pulled a fish from the water
And I got the shock of my life!!

A fella said that he had caught himself a whopper!
He'd cast out, and it gave him the come on,
And then after he had struggled to land it
He found that he'd caught a bloomin' big salmon!!

A man I know came home late after doing some fishing,
He said that he'd been caught up in a gale.
I asked him, "What has happened to your wellingtons?"
He replied," They were sucked off by a mighty big whale!!"

Two lads had gone out in a boat fishing,
And you should have seen the fish that they caught!
One said to the other, "Now you'd better mark this spot!"
So he put a cross on the bottom of the boat!!

Now fishing seems to be a very nice pastime,
But the fish I caught were a bit of a flop!
So I think in the future that I will just take a walk
And pay a visit to the fish and chip shop!!!

WHAT A YARN!

As I walked along the quay side, I saw an old fisherman.
He was repairing his nets with loving care
I said, "That looks awful tedious!" He looked up at me and smiled.
"Without these nets," he spoke. "I would have no food to bare!"

He was getting on in years, and his face looked tired and worn,
He wore a cap that was well faded with the sun.
He took a pipe from out his pocket, and then he sat down on the side.
"Take a pew!" he said. Then his tale began.

"It were when I was younger!" he spoke with glinted eye.
"One of my shipmates had bought himself a sailing craft.
He told me, 'I'm sailing to the Bahamas. If you'd like to come?'
And I said to him, 'Don't you think that's daft?'

"Well anyway, 'twas on a Monday morn when we hoisted up the sail,
And what a beautiful morning, the sky was vivid blue!
The water was like glass, and the wind was blowing fair,
And she was carrying a crew of twenty two.

"We'd been at sea for a couple of weeks, and everything was fine,
It was wonderful just listening to the wind in the sail.
Then suddenly from the mast there came a cry of 'avast!'
And then he called out that he thought he'd seen a whale!

"We all rushed on deck, he shouted, 'it's on the starboard side!'
And everyone scurried against the rail.
We all saw a water spout, then something hit us with a clout,
Then we rushed around collecting buckets, and began to bail!

"The ship began to sink, then I was washed into the tide,
But I managed to haul myself astride a piece of wood,
Then I drifted around the sea, and saw no one but me,
And then I fell asleep, as you thought I would!

"Now when I finally came around, I found I'd washed aground,
And I was laying on some beautiful deserted beach.
So I had a good scout around, I was on my own I soon found,
Then I came across some food that was growing within reach.

29

"A good few days had passed, when my heart started to beat fast -
In the sand a set of footprints, where someone's been!
And then through the trees was a band of women on their knees,
And they screamed I was the best lookin' fella that they'd seen!

"But instead of saying hello, I ran as fast as my legs would go,
And they cornered me as fast as your eyes can blink."
"So what happened?" I asked, "Don't keep me in suspense!"
"Oh, they ate me!" he smirked, "with a half cocked wink!"

I THINK I'M GETTING THE FLU!!

I'm feeling pretty miserable,
My head is spinning around,
My nose just won't stop running
And I hear a drumming sound.

My legs are beginning to tremble
And I can't bend to fasten my shoe,
I'm all hot and cold and shivering
Oh dear, I think I'm getting the flu!

I do my best to wrap up warm,
And be sensible in how I dress,
You don't know what to wear at times,
The weather's in such a mess!

You dress up for the winter,
And then the sky turns into blue,
You're wrapped up like a mummy
Then the steam starts hissing through!

You feel like a kettle that's boiling
But you can't lift off the lid,
Perhaps when we were born
We should have been fitted with a grid!

Then when you discard all your woollies,
The weather changes once again,
If it isn't the wind that howling
It's the rotten stinking rain!

And when you look after your body
Someone else carries the bug,
But instead of them staying indoors
They spread it like shaking a rug!

Now I'm not one for taking pills
Or filling up with drugs,
But there's times when you're feeling so rotten
That you say "To Hell!" and fill the jug!!

I don't know what I find is worse
The ailment or the cure,
But I'd like to think on this planet we live
That the air was a little more pure!

Now I'm not really a very old fella
But I look like I'm ready for my box!
If I take a couple more tablets
Then maybe I can reach my socks!!

It's awful when you're poorly
And all you want is hush,
But people think their being kind
When they call to make a fuss!

I like to think that I look tidy
When I'm laying on my bed,
Well, the doctor might just pay a call
And decide to pronounce me dead!!

MY COSTLY RASH!!

I visited my doctor the other day,
I found I'd broke out in a rash!
He made me take my clothes off
And then he asked me for some cash!!

"You look a little pale!" he said,
I said, "I've come on the National Health!"
He said, "I don't care if you've come by taxi,
I have got to make my wealth!"

I put into his hand a tenner
He said, "This will make you feel good!"
He stuck a needle in my backside
And then said that he wanted to test my blood!

He tied a tube around my arm
And my veins popped up plain as day,
Then he mumbled to himself,
"That's another fiver he will have to pay!"

He stuck a wooden thing into my mouth
And then he looked into my ear,
He stated, "Your eyes look pretty bloodshot!
Have you been on the beer?

"Perhaps if I give you a suppository
That will make you think!
But there again if you're slow on your feet
You could create a stink!

"When did the rash appear?" he asked.
I replied, "When I put on clean underpants."
"Tell your wife to give them an extra rinse!" he smiled.
"That's another fiver, next patient, and thanks!!"

YOU NEVER KNOW THE MINUTE!

I was walking down the street one fine evening
When quite suddenly I got plonked on the head!
And when I finally regained my consciousness
I found that I was laying on somebody's bed!!

Now this beautiful nurse was leaning over me
And she purred, "How are you feeling, OK?"
My head was spinning around like a top
And I couldn't tell her what was the day!

She purred, "You have taken quite a few knocks!
Can you tell me what happened last night?"
I said, "I was quietly walking down the street
When I was hit by an all lot of might!!"

Suddenly an old woman came into the room
And said, "I brought you in here last night.
Unfortunately it was me who knocked you on the head
And, boy, did it give me a fright!!"

She continued, "I was wiping over my window sill
When suddenly I came over all queer,
Then I knocked a plant pot off the ledge
And it hit you on the back of your ear!

"Well, you went down like a ton of bricks,
My God! I thought, he's dead!!
So I dragged you into the hospital
And they wrapped you up in bed!"

Now the nurse asked me, "What's wrong with your arm?"
And the old woman replied, "That's another story!!
As I was dragging him across the road
A fella backed over it with his lorry!!"

Then I let out a groan and said, "Oh my leg!!"
The old lady cried out, "I'm sorry that it's sore!
But when I dragged you over a garden
A man went over it with his mower!!

All of a sudden my jaw began to ache
And my eyes began to twitch.
Then the nurse who was looking at me quietly purred,
"I'm afraid you're in a bit of a fix!!

"Your body's in a state of shock,
You have certainly been through the mill!
Instead of this old lady helping you
I think she's been more prone to kill!!

"I will have to give you an injection," she added,
"Unfortunately it has to go in your bum!
But after it you won't feel the slightest of pain
Because all of your body will go numb!!"

The old woman gently pressed her hand into mine
And said, "I'll not go away, I will stay!"
Those were the last words I heard muttered
As I quietly passed away!!

I'VE JUST PASSED OVER!

I'm gone, I've just passed over, now I know I must be dead,
Because I'm floating like a ghost, while my body's on the bed.
I wasn't too good yesterday, I had an awful dizzy spell,
My wife said, "Have an early night, you'll soon be feeling well."

As I look down on my body, it's not a pretty sight,
I've gone all stiff and rigid, and my colour's ashen white.
My wife's just walked into the room. "C'mon, get up!" she cried.
And when she sees that I'm deceased, she throws her arms out wide.

"Oh dear, you've gone and snuffled it!" she cried, with anguish in her voice.
Your passing over's sudden, and you've left me with no choice.
I'll get a wardrobe kit from M.F.I. and ask Bill to redesign it,
Then screw four handles to the sides, I'll save myself a packet.

The doctor's next upon the scene, and has a fumble round.
"Yes, he's definitely gone!" he states, there's no pulse to be found."
He looked my body up and down, then said, "He's only a little feller.
I could have done with another pair of pants! What a pity he's not taller!"

Friends and relations all arrive, and gather around my bed,
They say how well I'm looking, and I shouldn't really be dead.
Bill's finished off his measuring, and said, "I guess it's there about,
But the nearest kit that I can get means his feet will be sticking out.

And then the vicar popped his head in. "By gum!" he quipped, "That was quick,
I thought I hadn't seen him around, but I didn't know he was sick.
Mind you, you're lucky my dear, this week's my special offer.
Instead of paying cash in hand, it's yours on the never, never."

They took me to the side of the grave, and then lay me on the floor,
And then lowered me down to the bottom, until I could go no more.
The vicar started muttering and said, "My soul redeem..."
Then suddenly I woke up sweating, it was all an awful dream.

I WAS RIDING PILLION

It was a lovely afternoon, as I sat on my own,
Beneath the shadows of a tree in the park
When I overheard crying, and soft gentle sighing,
From a young girl, who was breaking her heart.
I arose and walked over. I didn't want to alarm her,
And said, "Tell me please, what is making you sad?"
"My fiancé has gone!" she replied. "And left me alone,
I think that I made him upset and mad!

"We were going to a concert, he had bought the tickets.
We had both waited a long time to see the show,
But then on the night we had an awful big fight,
And he turned and walked out through the door!
But then on the next day he came back to say
That he would be leaving his home town for good.
I pleaded for him to stay or to take me away
Because my love for him he misunderstood.

"We roared off on his bike, the day was turned to night,
And the wind was shrieking all around.
They found him today on the ground where he lay
By his motor bike, that had a puncture they found,
Now he's gone on alone, and left me on my own,
I feel so lonely, and completely lost without him.

"But he hasn't gone for good, because I know he understood
That my heart will surely break without him."
"I am so sorry!" I said, as I slowly lowered my head,
It's so sad what has happened to you today!"
But I couldn't believe my ears, as she spoke through her tears,
"I was riding pillion!" she murmured, as her vision faded away.

STANDING CHARGES NEVER

Everything is paying out,
All I seem to get is bills,
It's money for this and money for that,
I should be a walking till!

Sometimes I don't know what I'm paying for,
And what's this standing charge?
How can you pay something for standing
When it's doing nowt by and large?

If a firm was to hire me
And all I did was to stand about,
They wouldn't pay me any wages
And they'd pretty soon kick me out.

You'd think people with a top education
Would put their skills to better use
Instead of working out ways to flannel us
And deprive us of our dues.

If I should be waiting for a taxi
And stood standing in a line,
Could the driver charge me extra
And call it standing time?

And if you're standing in a bus queue
Waiting for a bus,
Would you buy an extra ticket
For standing in the crush?

What if you were at the doctor's
Standing in the waiting room?
Would they supply you with extra treatment
To take away your gloom?

Standing charges! What a con!
Anything to get our money!
We have to pay or be cut off,
And that isn't very funny!!

They hung Dick Turpin for robbery,
But at least he wore a mask!
These people are taking us for all we have
And they don't even have to ask.

If my tap's turned off, and my well runs dry,
And there's nowt in my house to drink,
And I don't take a bath for months,
Then that will cause a stink!

Electricity, well that's a problem,
And so is my bloomin' gas!
But if I've nowt to make a spark with,
Then I can't cook my hash!!

The cost of bills never comes down,
They just spiral through the roof.
I say to these people, "stick your bills,
then you can stand aloof!!"

SAVING WATER

My wife stated, "Isn't it time you were taking a bath!"
I replied, "What am I celebrating today?
Anyway, I had a good bath at Christmas,
And it's only three months to the day!"

Now I think that I'm a pretty shrewd person
When the waterboard says "Save water today!"
I'm not a one who likes making a flood
While others are draining it away!

I consider myself a pretty clean person,
And if I bath once a year then I'm glad,
Mind, if I need one or not, I will still take the plunge,
But I don't think that I've ever smelled bad!

My wife makes a fuss over nothing
Because I always use plenty of soap!
And I scrub all the bits and important pieces
Including my cape of good hope!

She puts lots of water in the bathtub
And nearly always makes it too bloomin' hot!
I usually do a jig around the bathroom
With a steaming red ring around my bot!

The bubble-bath's a bit of a nuisance,
I'm usually all covered in foam,
And the bottom of the bath gets so slippery
That my feet wander off on their own!

I'd say hygiene was at the top of my agenda,
It has always given me a great sense of pride!
But I don't believe in the wastage of water
Because it might just stem the rise of the tide!!!

YOU CAN'T TAKE IT WITH YOU WHEN YOU GO

Some men collect money, some like valuables and gold,
Some collect penny blacks, and anything that's old,
Some collect paintings, and beautiful works of art,
But you can't take them with you, when you suddenly depart.

The world's full of collectors, people that like to hoard,
They'll push anything into a corner, to keep from feeling bored.
I saw a collection of antiques, just the other day,
And was told the previous owner, had sadly passed away.

Some people collect butterflies, and old vintage cars,
Some women collect thimbles, and fancy ornate jars,
Some men collect medals, and uniforms that catch the eye,
But you can't take them with you when you die.

The amount of second-hand shops show how the poor have sunk,
When they have to furnish their houses, with lots of worthless junk.
One old lady bought some chairs, she thought, "What a delight!"
Then when she went and snuffed it, their value tripled over night.

I was passing by an auction, not very long ago,
And the amount of people buying, I just couldn't believe it so.
The auctioneer held in his hands a pair of china dogs,
And respectfully told the bidders, the last owner had popped his clogs.

An artist has it pretty tough, while he's alive and kicking,
No-one's interested that he's painting for a living,
But as soon as he starts ailing, the crowds begin to gather,
And when he's laid beneath the ground, his work becomes a master.

Some men collect priceless art, while others collect trash,
Maybe at the end of the day, it all comes down to cash.
I had a collection once, but someone came and stole them,
Now when they find that they're deceased, they still can't take it with 'em.

41

FLY HIGH!

On a footpath, I quietly stood,
Watching an old lady gathering wood.
I called out, "Maybe I could give you a hand!
I'm doing nothing today that is planned."

She glanced at me sideways, and quietly replied, "Fine!
I don't mind your help, if it's not costing you time!"
I filled my arms with twigs, and waited for her to say,
"Now that we've finished, I will show you the way!"

But she had moved off without saying a word,
She must have walked quietly, not a footstep I heard.
I searched around, it seemed like hours on end,
And then I saw a tiny cottage, just around the bend.

At the back of the cottage, the old lady was stacking wood.
I quickly strode down to the place where she stood.
She looked up at me and said, "What took you so long?
I thought you'd got lost, but it looks like I'm wrong!"

"Where do you want these twigs?" I said with a smile.
"Put them inside!" she replied. "They'll last awhile!"
She took me inside the cottage, it was lovely and white,
And with the light from the window it really looked bright!

"That's the place for my twigs!" she said. "They will keep prime
Until I want to use them, it won't be for some time!
You've helped me no end!" she stated. "Please stay for tea,
I have some friends coming, and they would like to meet thee!"

Well, I felt surprised, I hadn't seen anyone near
And I couldn't imagine anyone being here!!
"How do they know?" I asked quite amazed.
"Oh, they've got the message!" she replied, with one eyebrow raised.

Well she set to baking, and my what a treat!
I just could not believe what she had made to eat!
"Now you get stuck in!" she said with a smile.
"My friends will come later, it will take them awhile!"

42

Well, I gulped down my tea at such a fast pace,
I felt uneasy, and wanted out of this place!
"Now you have a rest!" she quietly spoke.
"I will do the dishes, and then we can talk!"

Well, I must have dozed off, when I awoke with a jolt,
And I could see on the door, she had fastened a bolt!
I ran over to the window, and there in full swing
Was a band of witches, dancing in a ring!!

I rubbed my eyes and thought, this can't be true!!
Then the old lady appeared, as if out of the blue.
"Please don't be afraid!" she spoke with calm grace.
"I just want my friends to recognise your face!!

"These are good witches!" she spoke with a smile,
"And anyone who helps me, they help for awhile!
The twigs that you picked were so fine and dry,
And when I make brooms with them my friends will fly high!!"

"GERONIMO"

What gave man the urge to start flying
When God didn't supply him with wings?
And why put your faith in hot air balloons
That are not even fastened down with strings?

I know from the ground they look graceful,
And they certainly buzz along way up high!
But I don't fancy hanging in a basket
With nothing between me, the earth and the sky!

I'd be afraid of getting a puncture
And landing on someone's T.V. mast!
I couldn't imagine borrowing a bicycle pump
And a repair kit that's going to last!

The trouble is you can't even steer them!
They just tend to drift with the wind.
It's alright if you don't mind where you are going
But once you are up there you can't change your mind!

And what about when it starts raining?
Or maybe thunder and lightning should strike!
You can't very well hide under a table
Or run under the stairs out of sight!

And I don't know what clothes I should be wearing
Just suppose it could be freezing up there!
Maybe if I wore a set of woolly long johns
With a hot water bottle that everyone could share?

Now what if you wanted the bathroom?
You would have to wait an awful long time!
Especially if you wanted to go in a hurry
But the wind took you up in a climb!

Come to think of it there isn't that many haystacks
Or sand that stretches a very long way!
I would like to think that when I'm coming into land
That I will still be around for the next day!!

Well, I've seen them toss out the anchor,
But that doesn't mean where they'll end up!
What if you find that you're hanging from a tree?
or end up in a sty full of muck!!

For me hot air balloons just is not the answer
I like a bit of comfort instead!
It's nice to relax with a book in your hand
or to close your eyes, as if you're in bed!

Just to know what time you will be landing
And if you'll arrive all in one piece,
Just to know that the bathroom, isn't that far away
Brings to mind comfort and peace!!

I have never seen balloonists with parachutes,
Maybe they don't think about falling out!
But if they should drop out of the sky tomorrow,
Would "Geronimo" be the Indian to shout!!

MY FIVER

As I was walking down the street, I saw a fiver land on my feet.
I thought this is my lucky day, but a gust of wind blew it away.
I ran after it down the road, and it landed on a wagon's load.
The wagon halted at the very next street, and the fiver landed at a policeman's feet.

The policeman said, "Hello, hello," but as he stooped the wind did blow,
The fiver swirled around his feet, and then stuck on a bicycle seat.
The cyclist hadn't gone very far, when it blew off onto a moving car,
The driver saw it on the glass, and took his foot from off the gas.

He opened his door, and reached out for the cash,
But a bus swiped his door off, causing him to crash.
The wind lifted the fiver, and blew it away again,
It blew it over a bridge, and in front of a train.

The train blew its whistle, and pulled into a siding,
Then the fiver landed on a horse, that a young girl was riding.
She gave out a yell, the horse reared, then ran amok,
And the fiver landed on a fire-engine, that was attending some smoke.

The fireman thought he could reach it, if he pulled in his ladder,
But he got snagged up on a hose-pipe, and the fiver landed in the river.
An angler was reeling in his biggest catch for its size,
But when he saw the fiver, he dropped his top prize.

A blackbird flying low saw the angler's catch
And took the fiver in its beak with a daredevil snatch,
The bird soared high in the sky, then collided with a kite,
And down fell the fiver, it gave me a fright.

It floated past my face, and landed at my feet,
I couldn't believe my luck, it sure was a good luck streak,
I picked up the fiver, to put it with another I had!
But it wasn't there!! This fiver was mine! Boy, was I glad!

FIRST PAST THE POST!

I was invited on a day trip that was going to the races,
Now I'm not much of a gambling man, but I like a change of faces.
So I lated out my binoculars, and got myself some cash,
It's no good going to a racecourse, if you find you're short on brass.

A fellow sat behind me said, "I'm gonna make some money.
I'm gonna put a bundle on a horse called 'Sweet As Honey',
His form looks good, and his weight is right, I reckon he's a stayer."
I said, "They're not your horse's particulars! Your nag hasn't got a prayer."

He looked down at his paper, shouted "Grief!" then bit his lip.
"I gave a bloke a fiver!" he moaned, "to get that red hot tip."
A fella across said, "Don't worry, pal! I'll make us some bread.
It's all a matter of numbers, you've got to use your head.

"If one and one makes two and three and three aren't seven,
Then I reckon we've a winner, if we all back number eleven."
The fella that's sat beside me said, "How do you guess that's right?"
Then the other bloke jumped up and shouted, "That's it, we're gonna fight!!"

He threw a punch and missed him, and smacked a fella in front instead.
The fella turned around quite sudden, and belted him on the head.
And then the fella threw another blow, and hit a guy sat at the back,
Then he came lunging forward, and gave half a dozen a good smack.

Well, fists were flying everywhere, I got one on the head,
Then someone put the boot in, and kicked the driver instead.
The driver pulled the bus over, then shouted, "Bugger it all!"
And then leaped into the battle, making it a free for all.

Then when the fighting was over, and we all sat quietly back,
We all had a darned good laugh because it had been a real crack.
Then what a rotten day I had, every horse I backed got lost,
Mind, if I'd backed number eleven, it won at 40/1 first past the post.

BELT UP!

It was getting on for late one fine evening
And I was dashing about in a rush!
I was late, you see, and heading for home,
Well, I'd gone and missed the last bloomin' bus!

The street lights had gone out, I was blinkered,
Most of the streets were well in the dark,
Everything around was in total blackness,
I couldn't see a bloomin' bright spark!!

When quite suddenly from close behind me
I heard a real strange unnatural sound,
Like as though someone was following behind me,
As fast as lightning, I quickly spun around!

Not a sight or sound could I see of anyone,
And so I gingerly proceeded on my way,
But then again I heard this terrible grating
And my hair began to slowly turn grey!

I quickened my pace, and then started running,
But I could still hear that fearsome sound,
I ran into a doorway, with my eyes looking all ways,
There was still no one, only my heart on the ground.

I quickly moved along in the darkness,
But still that sound was following me there,
Then suddenly in my panic I stumbled over a small wall,
and landed on a patio chair!

I tugged and pulled, but I couldn't move it,
My bum was wedged well and truly in the seat!
I just couldn't believe my awful predicament
But I wasn't giving up in defeat!!

I was bent double as I ran at some railings,
And I gave the chair an awesome whack!
Then suddenly I was doing a somersault
And finished up, sprawled out on my back!!

If anyone had seen me they'd have thought me a contortionist,
And now my body was all racked in pain!
 But I'd only limped a few yards down the pavement,
When along came that terrible noise again!!

Then all of a sudden I walked into a lamp post,
And amidst all the darkness I saw stars,
Then in the gloom a bobby switched his torch on,
"By gum!" he said. "But you've been in the wars!"

"Come on!" he said. "I will light you homeward,
You can't see where you're going in this dark!"
But then again the noise started grating,
"It must be someone having a lark!"

The policeman escorted me to my gateway,
And then I took out the key to my door,
He then said, "Be careful that you don't trip over,
Your belts trailing," with the buckle dragging along on the floor!

WALKING

Someone suggested that I take up walking,
Well, I thought maybe I should,
So I started out on a pathway in a field
And ended up getting lost in a wood!

And then I seemed to be walking around in circles,
I just didn't seem to be getting far away,
Then suddenly I was surrounded by swarms and swarms of flies,
I felt like nothing was going right on this day!

I quickly beat a retreat into some bushes,
Then found that I was up to my neck in bloomin' nettles.
Now suddenly I was itching and covered in spots
And I wasn't feeling in very fine fettle!

Then I heard the frightening low hum of a nasty??
And so I ran for my life full of fear!
But then I stumbled head over heels
And the darned thing got me in the rear!!

Well, now I was feeling awfully rotten
And my back side was throbbing and sore,
I don't think this walking was cut out for me
And I definitely wouldn't do it any more!!

Then I followed a stream down to a crossing,
But thought I would jump over it instead,
I landed alright on the other bank
Then slipped back into the river bed!!

When I finally got back to where I started
Everyone gave out with a cheer,
And then they took me down the road for a pint
And I put a beer poultice on my rear!!

STEPS

Everywhere you go these days
You're either stepping up or down,
I can't understand the reason why,
It sure makes me wear a frown!

I notice people pushing wheelchairs,
Now that must be hard going.
One minute they're walking on solid ground,
And the next they find they're dropping

The blind must find things pretty tough
And all they carry is a cane,
One minute they're on solid ground
And the next they're in a drain.

I've seen women pushing kids in prams
And struggling down flights of stairs!
No one will think of giving them a hand
Or showing them how much they care!

When walking down most steps at night
I find they are always dimly lit.
Sometimes I can't see what I'm standing on -
Is it concrete, or am I on grit?

I feel sorry for all the people who have to struggle,
They are never asked to opinionate!
And when all the experts have finished
Then it's all too bloomin' late!!

My poor old socks are wearin' paper thin
And my legs are almost worn down!
I wish to heck I knew who was to blame
For all this stepping up and down!!

WELCOME TO MY HOME

Welcome to my home, my friend, won't you come inside?
Make yourself nice and comfortable, please sit down and bide,
How have you been keeping? It's nice of you to come!
Would you like a cup of tea and an ice covered bun?

How is the family doing? You should have brought them too.
We could have had a little party, a really good do!
The next time you find you're calling, please bring them along,
And we'll have a gathering, with a meal and a song!

Have you still got that problem or are you feeling better?
I went to see my doctor, because he sent me a letter.
I have to go to the hospital, to take a quick blood test,
I hope they don't take much from me, I haven't a lot at best!!

I'd decided to take up jogging, to get rid of some fat.
When I got as far as the front door, then I fell over the cat!
The cat let out one hell of a scream, and scarpered up the stairs,
Then my husband went and fell over him, now all I get is icy stares.

Well, now I'm on a diet, but it isn't all that good,
I'm not losing any weight, though I thought I would!
My bathroom scales, I find, just aren't up to scratch,
So I only eat between meals, then that way I can match!!

Now why are you crying my dear? Whatever's making you sad?
Oh' they're tears of happiness, then what's making you so glad?
What's that? You've won the lottery? An awful lot of money!
And you won't be visiting me again, but I mustn't think you're funny.

You're tired of my moaning, and you think that I'm a pain,
Now you've got that off your chest, you'll not be back again!
You say the money won't change you, you'll never be a snob
I say you'd better go right now before I smack you in the gob!!

SAME COLOUR DOOR!

Now I've just had a good night at my local
And the landlord has suddenly called out time!!
Mind, I'm glad because my legs have started to wobble
And my eyes aren't quite straight in a line!

I turned and said Goodnight to my buddies
And then I staggered out through the door,
Then when the fresh air has suddenly hit me
I've found I'm crawling along on the floor!

Now I've pulled myself up by a gatepost
And quietly staggered away down the street!
Straight into the arms of a policeman
Who is walking, patrolling his beat!

"Now then, young fella!" he muttered,
"I seem to know your face,
And I know that you don't live too far away,
But look at you, you're a disgrace!!

"Come on, I'll take you along with me!
Just show me the house where you stay.
I'll see you get home without any more fuss,
But I bet your wife will have something to say!!

He escorted me along on the pavement,
And my legs were all over the floor.
"This is the place I live, ossifer!"
I said, when I saw the colour of the front door!!

I struggled to find my front door key,
But it was missing from out of my mac!!
I said, "If you can point me around the corner,
Then I can climb over the back!"

Well, he took me around the corner,
And gave me a push up over the wall.
Suddenly I felt like Humpty Dumpty,
Even more so when I started to fall!!

"Are you alright?" shouted the policeman,
"I'm OK," I moaned, but I've flattened my hat!!
Then I went searching around on the doorstep
And found a key under the mat!

Now I let myself into the back kitchen
With one step forward, and three steps back!!
Then I fell over some 'at t'other side of the doorway,
And gave myself a hell of a crack!!

Now I managed to struggle to the stairway
And I pulled myself up one at a time!
Then I quietly staggered into the bedroom,
Boy, that was one hell of a climb!!

Well now, I got into bed with my socks on
And put my arms around the woman I'd missed.
Time passed, then someone suddenly put the light on,
And it looks like someone else's wife I've just kissed!

RIGHT UP YOUR FLUE

As I walked down the street, I heard a complaining
From an old lady, who was scrubbing her stair.
"Just look at all this rubbish, and grime that I'm cleaning
I'd like to catch the so-and-so, who keeps leaving it there!

"There's cigarette ends, and all them empty packets,
They trail all the way up to the end of the street.
But you never see the folk who leave all this garbage,
They must wait till it's dark, and drop it discreet.

"Their homes must be filled up to the rafters
With rubbish and trash they don't clear away.
Why don't they get rid of it, like caring people,
Instead of waiting for others, to clean it away?

"I have no time for those loathsome people,
They're dirty, lazy, inconsiderate and all,
They take their dogs out, it's now time for walkies,
They run up the street, and pee on my wall.

"They think that its funny, watching them performing,
Like it's a circus animal doing a trick,
The dog should be squirting on its owners property,
They he wouldn't be amused, because it would make them sick.

"I clean down my paintwork, with plenty of scrubbing,
Then stand in a deposit, that sticks to my shoe,
I don't see the sense in these people having animals,
I'd like to put my foot right up their flue!!"

I'D RATHER STAY AT HOME!!

I remember once staying in a caravan
My wife said she had booked it for a week.
It was the longest week of my entire life
And, boy, did it make me want to weep!!

I don't think it ever stopped raining,
And it was stuck in the middle of a field.
The noise was like skeletons dancing on the roof
With the caravan acting as a shield!

And then flies came swarming by the millions,
They must have thought it was a Five Star Hotel.
And then to empty the waste, I had to plough through the mud,
To me it was worse than A Y.M.C.A. hostel!!

The heating and cooking was by calor gas
And by heck it didn't half stink!!
I remember my wife cooking food on the stove,
We thought something was wrong with the sink!

Our children all had to wear wellies,
Mind, they thought they were really good,
I'd started to grow webs between my toes,
Well, I really thought that I would!!

On one of the nights I thought I'd take a shower,
But they were all vandalised and broke,
And when I went back out into the weather
They had to pull me out of the mud with a rope!!

Now I'm not a one for spoiling people's pleasure,
But they really do give me a pain,
And the only thing that I would use a caravan for
Is to keep chickens in out of the rain!!

I LIKE RIDING MY BICYCLE

I like to ride my bicycle
But I never really go very far,
Well, I might just end up getting lost
Or being knocked off by a car!

The roads are so very busy now,
I find it difficult to even ride in the street.
No sooner that my feet are on the pedals
than my backside's being knocked off the seat!!

I was cycling down the road just the other day
When a motorist opened his car door,
And even before I knew what was happening
I was laying flat out on the floor!!

Now a young fella dashed over to help me
"By heck!" he said. "That was a real hard sock!"
And there I was laying in a poor crumpled heap
In a terrible state of shock!!

The driver as usual looked stupid.
"Sorry, I didn't see you!" he said.
Maybe I should ride covered in flashing lights
With a tin hat covering my head!!

The young fella helped me back to my house
And my wife gave him a fiver for his trouble.
I couldn't give him anything at all
Because all I was seeing was double!!

Then after he'd left, my wife said, "What a nice lad!
There's not many kind people on this patch!"
I glanced at my wrist and said, "You've nearly got it right,
But he's just buggered off with my watch!!"

I'M LIKE A TURTLE WITH ONLY ONE SHOE!

I have never thought about taking up running,
It's my legs, they're not much to go on at all!
When I look down, they're pretty scrawny and skinny
And they don't really make me look tall!

Not long ago, I remember missing the last bus
And I chased it to the bottom of the street.
then I collapsed on the ground gasping,
And I found that I was well and truly beat!

Mind, I can run if someone is chasing me
And you can't see my legs for dust!
I'm like a ferret as it shoots down a rabbit hole
But my lungs are almost ready to bust!

I put my name down for a long distance school run
That happened a very long time ago.
Everyone had gone home when I had finished
So I won a prize for being the slowest of the slow!!

I once remember someone having an accident,
And they were in such terrible pain.
By the time I'd got someone to help them
They said that they were feeling okay again!!

I knew a fella who was a bookie's runner,
But I never saw him dashing about,
Until one day, he ran off with the takings,
And then he found that his time had ran out!!

No, I've never been a great one for running,
But I admire the people who do,
Especially if they win lots of races,
Me, I'm like a turtle with only one shoe!!

I WILL NEVER DANCE NO MORE!

I thought that I would take up dancing
But I wasn't very good,
Trying to learn the dance steps
Was like knocking my head against wood!

One two three, one two three,
And then I went on to five,
I was trying to dance to a waltz
But people thought I was doing the jive!!

A fella said that I would be all right,
If I could just count the beat,
I was all right doing the counting
But suddenly I had two left feet!!

I started doing the Dashing White Sergeant,
And thought, "Well now! This is rather neat,
But suddenly I lost my footing
And a Gay Gordon helped to me feet.

He said, "There there now! You're all right, dear,"
And then he showed me how to twirl,
But I got myself into a rare old spin
And then landed in the lap of a girl!!

"Oh!" she cried. "You are light on your feet!
I have been watching you all night."
But when I saw that she had no teeth in
it gave me one hell of a fright!!

I gave her a quick "Excuse me,"
And tap danced out of the door,
Then while tripping along the pavement I vowed
I would never dance no more!!

SKINNY AS A LATH

Now I'm not a keep fit fanatic,
Or someone who likes running around,
I'm just a fella who enjoys a nice quiet walk
And I'd never let myself be house-bound!

No, I'm not one who drops down into press-ups
Or hoists anything over my head!
I would sooner walk in the sunshine
Or have a lovely meal instead!

I've seen lots of folk running around jogging,
But I wouldn't do that, even for a bet!
I know when I've had them jog past me
That I've suddenly broken into a sweat!!

When I see all the musclemen on the beaches,
Then I suppose that my body looks tame!
But I'd rather be the way that I am
Than to be taking things to stay in the game!!

I knew a fella who was after the perfect body.
He said, "The tablets I take, I know I can trust!"
One day I saw him waddling down the street
And he was sporting a forty eight bust!!

I have a bicycle, and I've had it some time now,
But I don't like going out in the rain!
Mind; it's exercise when I'm pumping the tyres up
And watching them go down again!!

No, I've never been a keep fit fanatic
But I like to think that I'm not over fat!
A bit of walking is what I like doing,
Mind, I'll never be as skinny as a lath!!

I'LL HOLD MY BREATH IN!!

Why is it I was born very skinny?
Why wasn't I born looking fat?
When I'm dressed, all my clothes just hang off me,
And I feel like I'm nothing but a lath.

By bones stick out just like a skeleton's!
I have never seen anything as thin.
My legs make me look like a sparrow
And my kneecaps, the dimples are bigger on my chin!!

Now I'm afraid to walk on the pavement
In case I should fall down a crack!!
My legs are so awfully skinny
I'm afraid I could never climb back!!

A butcher said that he had seen more meat on a pencil!!
Well, I took that as being a slight,
But seeing that he was a much bigger fellow
I didn't invite him to come outside and fight!!

So I thought that I would take up weight-lifting,
I fancied pumping iron to give me more might!
But when I stripped off ready to start pumping
Everyone fell about laughing at the sight!!

Then I decided to try weight-gaining tablets
And I filled up with yeast and the like,
Until one day I was going to the chemist
And a motorist knocked me off my bike!!

He said that he hadn't even seen me!!
I replied, "Well, I don't know that I'm bloomin' well thin!
But even that doesn't make me invisible,
The next time I'll hold my breath in!!

BOY, DID I LOOK A SIGHT!

When I'm dressed up I like to feel comfortable,
But everyone says my clothes are out of date!
I don't wear them to be a trendy in fashion,
I just wear them to have a feeling of first rate!

Now I don't mind people holding opinions,
Just as long as they keep them to themselves.
I don't criticise other people's sense in dresswear
Though some look like they've fallen off a shelf!

I had a wonderful old pair of comfortable slippers,
And for years they served me a faithful role.
Then one day I went over the doorstep - it had been raining -
That's when I found to my horror, they had no sole.

I had a jumper that was especially knitted for me
And I'd had it for many long years.
My wife said, "I'll wash it for you, don't worry!!"
But it grew, and I was reduced to tears.

I used to wear a pair of drainpipe trousers,
But when dancing they decided to separate!
I fell head over heels onto my backside
And everyone thought I was trying to demonstrate!

I had a powder-blue finger tip jacket,
Then one day when I was riding my bike
I flew off while taking a corner
And me and my jacket ended up in a dyke!

I mislaid a suit, then found it in a suitcase,
So I thought that I would wear it that night.
Unknown to me the moths had held a banquet,
It fell to pieces and, boy, did I look a sight!!

I'M NOT REALLY A PRUDE!

I have applied for a job as a model!
Well, I thought that I'd give it a try.
I'm a very smart-looking fella
When I am wearing a suit and a tie.

Now I know that I'm not very tall,
But perhaps that doesn't matter.
I can always wear some built-up shoes
Or swing off the top of a ladder!

They didn't say anything about handsome,
The word they came up with was "mature".
Now I know that I'm not all that pretty,
But being aged is one thing that I'm sure!

I hope they're not wanting slim fitting!
Cos my body's not in the greatest of trim,
But I suppose if I hold in my stomach,
Then I might look a little bit more thin!!

It's taken me years to build up my body,
Now one or two bits have started to sag.
And when I look at my face in the mirror
Maybe I should wear a paper bag!!

My legs aren't my greatest asset,
They're not much to go on at all,
The only thing I can say in their favour is
That if I stumble, then I don't have far to fall!!

Now they haven't told me what I'd be modelling,
But I hope that it's nothing that is rude.
I wouldn't like folk to get the wrong idea,
But there again, I'm not really a prude!!

I'M GOING TO GET MY HAIR CUT

I'm going to get my hair cut, it's starting to look a sight.
It looks awful when it's sticking up, as though I've had a fright.
I haven't got a lot on top, it's getting pretty thin at best,
And looking on with reflection, I seem to have more on my chest.

I just can't see the reason, for having hair growing out of my head,
To me it's just a nuisance, I'd rather wear a hat instead.
With all this excess fungus, and having to pay to get it cropped,
You only need to buy one hat, either flat or one that's topped.

My barber's a pretty decent chap, and he isn't all that dear,
He has in-depth knowledge of what's going on around here.
I suppose I can save a bob or two, if I didn't buy a paper,
Then he can tell me all the news, and keep me in the picture.

Sometimes he chats about football, and he seems to know about cricket,
He talks about the government, in fact he know's no limit.
He only has a little place, it's always clean with no smoking!
You'd be hard pressed with a fag in your mouth to try to do the talking.

He has all kinds of customers, short and long, thin and fat,
Most want a short back and sides, others want to look like a rat.
Some of them have lots of hair, others like me it's quite rare,
One or two move it around a bit, to hide where it's barren and bare.

I've never thought about wearing a toupee, to me that's like wearing a hat,
And if you catch anything in it, it would be like shakin' a mat!!
I'm not a big one for vanity, but I like to look well turned out,
And if it only means getting a haircut that's nothing to shout about.

So I've decided to get my haircut, I hope I'm the first in the chair,
I don't want to be hanging around, I want to be away from there.
Well, I've been to get my haircut, he'd be open, I supposed,
But when I reached the barber's, I found that he was closed!!

MONDAY OF NEXT WEEK!

Oh dear, the alarm clock's ringing!
It's time I was getting out of bed.
I thought I could hear a loud buzzing
Going around inside of my head!

It doesn't seem like five minutes ago
When I laid my head down for a nap,
And now it's time that I was getting up
I could just go around another lap!

Now I had a couple of drinks last night
And my head's spinning around like a top!
But if I don't make it into work
Then I'm heading for the chop!!

I just can't seem to get my shirt on,
Oh, the darned things inside out!
And now I've gone and lost a button,
What the heck's it all about?

The socks I've found don't match up,
And one of them has got a hole!
Maybe if I wear them inside out?
Then they won't get noticed at all!!

Just wait a mo', what's happened 'ere?
I only seem to have one leg!!
And I'm hopping around the bedroom
Just like Jake the Peg!!

Now where is my other slipper?
It has to be under the bed!
If I can just stretch a little further -
There, now I've gone and banged my head!!

I've had to hobble to the bathroom,
And my head is spinning around!
But now that I've taken a couple of aspirins
I will soon by feeling better, I'll be bound!

I have given myself a darned good wash
And now I feel a whole lot better
Suddenly I've slipped going down the stairs!
I thought I was on a helter skelter!

My feet have buckled under me
And I've landed on my chest!
I think that I'll stay where I've fallen,
I guess I'm ready for a good rest!!

Now all my poor old bones are aching,
I just wish that I was bloomin' well dead.
I think that my body has given up its ghost,
Well, I should have stayed in bed!!

I've struggled to get my coat on,
When the newspaper lands at my feet!
And on the front it reads "Sunday!"
I'm not in work until Monday of next week!!

SECOND ON THE LEFT, THEN FIRST RIGHT

One of the major stores was holding a sale.
My wife stated, "I want you to be first in the door!"
She wanted me to sleep on the pavement all night
So I'd be ready to walk into the store!

She told me I had to get myself prepared!
And the suite was on the second floor,
So I'd better get myself a good sleeping-bag
And a flask, with hot coffee galore!

Well, I bought myself a transistor radio
And a pair of woolly socks for my feet,
A balaclava to keep my ears from tingling,
And a pair of long johns, with a patch in their seat!!

And then around came the night of my action!
Yes I was all dressed up and rarin' to go.
When I arrived, I was the only one waiting by the doorway,
And then it suddenly started to snow!!

It rained and it hailed, and then it pelted down,
Then my transistor wouldn't work at all.
I spilled half my coffee in the sleeping-back
And my sandwiches were just a soggy ball!

I awoke and found I was solid with cramp
And a dog showed his winkle to me!
I was wet through, frozen, and as stiff as a board
And covered in stinking dog pee!!

Then suddenly I recognised the store manager
"Don't hold me up!!" he screamed into my face.
A policeman ran down the street towards us
And stated," Don't you know you're in the wrong place?

"Your wife asked me to keep an eye on you!
But unfortunately I was taken ill last night.
The store you want is just around the corner,
Second on the left, then first right!!"

SNORING!!

My wife tells me that I am always snoring
And that I sound like a dirty great pig!!
Now that's why around two thirty in the morning
She gives me an awful sharp dig!!

Now I can't say that I've heard myself snoring,
I have only her word to go on!
Mind, I've woken myself up a couple of times
And I can't imagine that I've been singing a song!!

But sometimes she isn't all that understanding -
I mean, I could have a medical condition!
But all that she does is to knock me about,
Encouraging my wailing rendition!!

Mind you she has got a bit of a temper
And sometimes I get a real tongue lashing!
I wouldn't mind her wearing those kinky black boots,
And then she could really give me a thrashing!!

But deep down I know that she loves me,
It's just she has a strange way of letting me know!
Most wives make their husbands a nice iced cake
With powdered glass that looks like snow.

Now I'm not saying that we're not compatible,
There's many a time we've seen eye to eye!
But she says that is she hears me snoring again
Then I'm going to find myself sleeping in a sty!!

SHE IS A GOOD SHOT!!

I have not got a nagging wife
Just one who moans a lot.
I don't think that she really means it
Because I'm all that she's bloomin' well got!!

Now she likes me to be here at meal times
And I have not got to be late,
One time something happened, and I was a little overdue,
And she hit me over the head with a tin plate!!

Well, I have a very understanding wife,
She seems to understand me a lot!
When she says, "Understand what time to be in!"
Then she states, "Just understand it's ten o'clock!!"

But when I'm working around the house
She always makes me a nice cup of tea!
And then she'll say, "Don't take too long over that!
I want you out of my way you see!!"

Now our son emigrated to America,
I think he did it to get our of her way!
But if ever I forget something, and answer her back,
Then I have hell to pay!!

I bought my wife a new washing machine,
The old one just coughed twice, and died!
But the time it takes for the new one to wash,
We could both be on the other side!!

But when I think about my wife, I can't grumble!
It could have been a darned sight worse for my lot!
There's a fella who lives a couple of doors down the street,
His wife throws plates, and she's a crack shot!!

JUST WAIT UNTIL THEY'VE GONE!

It's washing day, them's the words I don't like!
My wife starts running around like someone not right.
The beds all get stripped, and the curtains come down,
And the poor old canary gets turfed upside down!

"Have you any dirty washing?" My wife calls from below!
"I have put it in the basket!" I call back in echo.
"What are you wearing?" Her voice sternly enquires.
"I have put on clean slacks, and a shirt that's expired!"

The next thing I know, she's dashing up the stairs.
"We have visitors coming!" she cries. "You will have me in despair!
Put on something nice, what about a white shirt?
But keep out of the garden, away from the dirt!

"And wear a nice tie, that will make you look smart!
But nothing too fancy, you have to look the part."
"The tie that you like," I said, "you washed it last week,
And the last time I saw it, well, it looked like a wet leek!"

"Oh dear!" she said blushing. "Then put on a jersey."
"The one I like," I replied, "has gone loose and baggy!"
"I put it in the spin drier," she said, "to keep it all together,
And then I hung it out, it must have been the weather!"

"Put on your cardigan, then!" she said. "That's quite fetching."
"I can't!" I replied. "I have put it in the washing!"
"Well you'd better find something, anything will do!
Our visitors will be here in a minute or two!!

The door bell rang, my wife flew down the stairs.
I came down a little later, to face up to her glares.
I'd taken my cardigan out of the wash and then put it on,
But the look on her face said, "Just wait until they've gone!!"

WHO'S GOT WHAT?

We've bought another washing machine, the old one's given up and died.
The engineer came out to look at it, he just broke down and cried.
"It's dead!" he said, as he shook his head. "It's past all redemption."
It never caused me any problems, and hardly needed any attention.

"But I don't know about your new one!" he stated, as he cleared his throat.
"It isn't build like the old one, I don't think it will last like it ought.
Most of it's made out of plastic, and the rest of it's made out of tin.
Mind, if you find it's not doing the washing, it'll make a good dustbin.

"That's the quality you buy these days, there's nothing built to last.
Before they reach their sell-by date, they've given their last gasp.
So I'll fix it up, and plug it in, and watch while it goes.
I hope it does your washing, and doesn't pass into death throes."

Well, he turned it on and away it went, the clothes spun round and round,
 But when we took the washing out, only one sock could be found.
He stripped the bloomin' washer down, but couldn't find the other,
But found a pair of knotted tights, that belonged to someone's mother.

"That's strange!!" said the engineer, "It's supposed to be a new machine.
How can washing go missing, and tights appear that we've never seen?"
He stripped it down once again, and came up with a pair of briefs,
"I can't believe what's happening," he said, "it's all beyond belief."

Then he took a spanner, and had everything in bits,
He found my sock all chewed up, and a pair of pants covered in grit.
And then he found a tablecloth, and sheets coated with grease,
With a couple of fifty pences, so we both had one apiece.

And then the front door bell rang, it was the manager from the store.
"I'll have to take the washer back!" he said, "and what is more,
It belongs to a woman in this street, who put it in for repair,
It wouldn't give back all her washing, and now her washer isn't there!"

FOLK THAT CAN'T LEAVE NOTHING ALONE!

Why is it that some folk have just got to tamper?
They just can't leave anything alone!
When they hear a radio, and they're not happy with the sound
Then they just have to make it groan!!

Nothing is sacred to these meddlesome people,
They have always got to fiddle and touch,
And when they have broken something, or knocked it for six,
All you hear is, "That can't have been very much!!"

They love to play around with anything that's mechanical,
Out come the screwdriver and spanner.
And when they find out that it no longer works,
They always make a hasty departure!

All types of engines always seems popular,
You'll always see someone having a fiddle!
The chap at the garage only told me last week,
The last engine he saw he thought was a riddle!!

They must spend hours just taking things to pieces
And giving them a good looking over.
I know of someone who took a TV to bits,
He build another from the pieces left over!!

A fella I know bought himself a speedboat
He messed around to make it go faster!
Then one day while cruising he suddenly took off
And his trip ended up in disaster!!

But there's nothing we can do about these meddlers,
Everything they touch, they just break!
But I want to say, "Please keep your hands off,
And leave things alone, for heaven's sake!!"

MY MISSUS IS PRICELESS!!

Now why was woman put on this earth?
Was it just to torment man?
Because most of the things, that I seem to do
Never work to a woman's plan!!

I can never just seem to get things right!
And at times I am only being helpful!
But then my wife starts up an argument
And everything becomes eventful!

Now when my wife comes down with a tantrum
Then, by gum I have got to watch out!!
And when her hands fly about all over the place
She has often landed me with a clout!!

There's nothing worse than a woman's scorn!
Them's words, that I have oft times heard.
But I reckon that whoever said them,
His wife's hearing must have been impaired!!

Now my wife can lip-read around corners!
I have never known her to miss a trick
And when I am working in the garden,
She doesn't help me one lick!

I'm the one who cleans all the windows
And works hard on the D.I.Y. chores,
And woe betide me if I'm found on the patio
Because she's been drawn to my side by my snores!!

And she says that I should bathe more often,
Then plays hell, if I don't clean out the bath!!
I'm slowly becoming a nervous wreck
Because of this woman's terrible wrath!!

Now I'm not a fella who goes looking for trouble,
Because it's never too far to be found,
And I find that if my wife should be that way out,
Then I don't want to be hanging around!!

But I'll tell you this woman is a darned good cook!
She can knock anything up in a trice.
And when it comes down to washing the pots
She says, "I will not be telling you twice!!"

Now she has a specific place for the dishes,
But I don't know where they all go.
Yet I can easily tell when she's getting upset,
Because I always feel the point of her toe!!

Mind, she does very well with the shopping,
Because to me that's a bloomin' awful task!
But when she starts to grumble about the prices
That is when I am afraid to ask!!

But for all that I have to say about my missus,
I wouldn't swop her for all of the earth!
Because when we are snuggled together by the fireside
To me nothing could equal her worth!!

SHE'S A TRAMP

She doesn't love him, she keeps him on a string,
He buys her flowers, because it's the done thing,
She has an apartment, but he pays the dough,
She's a tramp, and likes to keep him in tow.

She visits night clubs, and strings him right along,
He buys her drink all night, she pay him with a song,
The man adores her, and to him she can't do wrong,
But she's a tramp, and he won't say, "So long!"

She has her hair done at the best salons,
And her dresses she never buys in ones,
Her jewellery is the very best in town,
She's a tramp, but it doesn't get him down.

She's a queen, he's put her on a throne,
The way she treats him, he'd be better off alone,
Love is precious, and not to be abused,
But she's a tramp, and all men are there to be used.

She has no respect, and takes what she can,
And with her body, it's all taken from man,
He gives her money, and everything that's around,
She's a tramp, and grinds him into the ground.

She's a selfish and pure conceited gal,
The sort of woman you don't want as a pal.
She'll pick your bones clean, then come back for your eyes,
She's a tramp, and I ain't telling you no lies.

The woman's evil, and rotten to the core
When she has everything, she'll still come back for more,
But the man loves her, and he can't break the spell,
She's a tramp, and she makes his life a living hell!!

A PAIN IN MY UNMENTIONABLE!

As I quietly look out of my window
I can see lots of frost upon the pane,
Now I know that Jack Frost has landed
And it's winter time once again!

Everything out there looks frozen,
I don't think that I'll venture past the door.
The last time I walked upon icy ground
I finished up laying on the floor!

But I must say it really looks a picture,
With those icicles hanging low!
I don't suppose it will be very long now
Before we're having lots of snow!

Snow always looks nice on Christmas Cards
Or when you see it pure white on the street!
But it isn't half bloomin' awful to walk in,
And just look at what it does to your feet!!

No, for me winter isn't the best of our seasons!
I much prefer summer instead.
At least we get a little bit of sunshine
And everything isn't frozen or dead!!

Mind I must admit that I like Christmas,
With all its warmth and good cheer!
Maybe it's the time when people say, "Hello!"
That makes me glad Christmas is here!

But winter with its awful blooming weather
Is something that we can all do without.
It just gives me a pain in my unmentionable
Every time I have to go out!!

JUST ONE OF THOSE DAYS

The sky's shedding tears. Oh dear, it's pouring with rain!
I've put on a coat, my umbrella's sticking again,
I have forced the thing open, now some spokes have got bent,
A small hole has appeared. Suddenly it's a great bloomin' rent.
I've scavenged around, and I've found an old hat,
But when it's on my head, it looks like a dead rat!
Mind, anything's better than getting wet through.
Now I've ventured forth, and found a hole in my shoe.
My foot's rotten sodden, and water's running down my neck,
Now I'm feeling all wretched, a saturated wreck!
I'm trying to find shelter, as I dash past a puddle,
But my feet slip on the ground, now I know I'm in trouble.
As I sit in the water, all dripping wet through,
A passer-by helps me up, now I'm really in a stew!
I offer them my thanks, and then hurry on my way,
I must look a sight, I'm in such disarray.
My trousers are soaking, and my coat is wet through,
Now I've started sneezing, I must be getting the flu!
It's my wife's fault I'm here, in this terrible wet,
She made me venture forth, a present to get.
The shop manager glanced at me, with a look of disdain,
He thinks I'm seeking shelter, just to get out of the rain!
"You can't stand in here!" he shouts out with regret,
"Because you are making my carpet all soaking wet!"
I glanced at his face, it was a picture of scorn,
It's times like this when I wish I wasn't born!
Then an assistant appears, looking cheery and bright,
"It's all right, sir!" she calls out. "It was picked up last night!!"
So I turned to the door, all steaming wet through,
And looked up to the sky, it's now a beautiful blue!!

HEINZ'S FIFTY SEVEN

I got up early in the morning, and struggled out the door,
It isn't very funny, when it's peeing down or more.
I made my way along the pavement, and bought a paper on my way,
"It's another rotten morning!" I can hear someone say.
I dodged half a dozen puddles, as I moved along the street,
A little Heinz's Fifty Seven started snapping around my feet.
I walked a little faster, to try to shake the blighter loose,
But it made him more determined as I stepped out like a goose.
I approached the edge of the pavement, now I had to cross the street,
But the Heinz's Fifty Seven was still snapping at my feet.
A car came in a little close, near the spot where I was stood,
And me and the Fifty Seven looked as though we'd been through a flood.
I looked down, and he looked up, and then he shook himself dry,
Then once again he grabbed my trouser leg, and really let fly.
I decided I would take a chance and ran across the street,
But that little Fifty Seven was still clinging to my feet.
I safely reached the other side, and there stood a woman on her own,
She cracked me with her brolly, and cried, "Leave that poor dog alone!"
My head started aching, as I ran along the street,
But that little Fifty Seven was still hanging around my feet.
I dashed around the corner, straight into the arms of P.C. Charm.
"Hey! hang on! What's your hurry?" he cried, as he grabbed me by the arm.
"I'm late for work!" I told him, as I continued on my way.
"Where's that dog's lead?" he shouted. "He's not mine!" I echoed. "He's just a
bloomin' stray!"
I turned my head and suddenly I was laying on the floor,
Because some silly dizzy nit had opened a car door.
The little Fifty Seven thought that it was all a game
And bit me on the backside, so I called him a very rude name.
I got up, and ran along the pavement, until I reached my place of work,
And the little Fifty Seven followed closely in my wake.
A security guard appeared, and began locking up the gate.
He said, "They've all walked out and gone on strike, you missed them 'cos you're
late!!"
I picked up the Fifty Seven, he gave a little moan,
And shoved him inside my coat. I had decided to take him home.

78

WORSE THAN A DEAD HORSE

I was watching fellas working on a building site,
By gum, they worked bloomin' hard.
They seemed to be up and down ladders all day
And pushing wheelbarrows all around the yard.

One fella carried bricks on his shoulder,
Another was digging a trench,
One of them was stacking breeze blocks
While another was mixing cement.

The foreman came out of his cabin
Carrying a tape measure and pencil in his hand,
He strode over to a house in the corner
And shouted, "This isn't how this building was planned!"

He measured the front door with his tape measure
And then stood back shaking his head.
"What happened to the window?' he called out.
"You've put a bloomin' door there instead."

He entered the house and then vanished,
And a scream echoed back through the door,
Followed by a host of bad language
And, "Where the heck's that so-and-so floor?"

I dashed over to see if I could help him,
He groaned, "There's music coming out of that hole."
We both peered into the cavity
And could see a radio bricked into the wall.

"Oh, you can't get the labour that you used to,"
He muttered. "All they do now is go on a course,
And then they call themselves builders.
I reckon they're worse than a dead horse."

THE CUCKOO CLOCK

Our cuckoo clock fell off the wall
And now he makes no sound at all!
All is peaceful in our house
You can almost hear a tiny mouse!

We miss his chirpy call on the hour,
He was never right, but it didn't matter.
Now we just have a nail in the wall
And that doesn't tell the time at all!

When he fell, he made such a clat,
With a quick "Cuck," and "Oo!" Then that was that!
Well, now I'm trying to get him repaired
But it looks like his poor old cuckoo's impaired!

We have had the clock for quite a while,
And he has always managed to make us smile.
It will be sad if this is his demise,
That's why we are hoping that like the phoenix, he will rise!

I can't imagine burying a clock,
Although I might say we have a decent plot!
I buried a canary once, that was sad,
Mind, when he was covered, he didn't look too bad!

Now we're hoping that we won't have the loss,
Particularly my wife, she won't half be cross!
Well, I bought the clock for her, you see,
It was for her Anniversary.

And it was me who knocked it off the wall,
So now I get no peace at all.
Mind, she could always hang me from the nail,
I can't "Cuckoo" but I can certainly wail!

A SAD TALE!

I heard a real sad tale in the shipyard
About a fella who's luck was down the nick.
He'd just started work on the Monday
And he didn't have two pennies to click!

Now the lads all got together a collection
To try and help this fella through.
Mind, they tell me that he tended to pong a bit,
So someone bought him some soap and shampoo!

And then he was given a haircut
Round the back where they cut up the cork,
But they say that he wasn't very happy
Because it looked like they'd used a knife and fork!!

Then he was given a pair of decent trousers
And a jacket that was too good for work!
A packet of fags and some matches
With a hat. That made him look a berk!!

Someone fitted him up with a cardigan
But he found it a little bit tight.
Anyway, he said that he wouldn't be found dead in it
Because it made him look too much of a sight!

Well anyway, he just happened to be walking across the shipyard
When his shoe sole began flapping about!
And a manager who just happened to be passing
Hailed him with quite a loud shout!!

"That could be dangerous!" the boss indicated,
And took a wad of notes out all brand new!!
He then removed the elastic band from around the money
And said, "Here you are! Put that around your shoe!!"

SEEING IS BELIEVING?

My father was a medium,
People have said he was pretty good!
But I don't know if he heard the rattle of chains
Or a constant knocking on wood!

I wouldn't say I'm not a believer!
But there again seeing is believing and that's the truth!
I can't say I've seen anything move by itself,
Somebody's usually given it a push!

I was once stood on a ladder
And the rung beneath my feet suddenly broke!
But instead of falling to the concrete below
I went up in the air and felt choked!

I've always thought that I have a guardian angel!
There's somebody looking over my head.
My life has been lucky in more ways than one,
Or maybe it's the way that I've made my bed?

My grandmother used to tell fortunes,
She'd read tea cups or lines on your palm.
I don't know if she knew what she was doing
But she really didn't mean any harm!

Quite a few people say they have psychic power,
Now should I believe them or not?
I think just as long as they're happy in their belief
Then they're better left alone with their lot!

We still need quite a bit of understanding
About things going around in our head.
My grandma told me, "It isn't the deceased who will harm you in life,
It's the living that's trying to make us all dead!!!

I'M A COMMITTEE MAN!!

Now I like a game of snooker on a Tuesday night,
But early the other evening, my night was turned into a blight.
A fella called out to me," I don't want to sound unjust,
But while you're playing snooker, I won't have you eating nuts!"

"Nuts!" I said. "Nuts!" he replied. "Don't take the Mickey out of me!
You are making me look foolish, and that is plain to see.
We have rules and regulations for what goes on in here.
You can't be chewing nuts. That's eating, not drinking beer!"

"But how can eating nuts upset you?" I asked him with a frown.
"Do as you're told!" he mumbled. "Don't make me out a clown!
You have vandalised the tables, the place is a disgrace!!
Men have salt on their balls, with grease all over the place.

"You can't play a game of snooker whilst slipping here and there,
And if your opponent has salty balls, then it really isn't fair!
I'm saying now for all you've done, you really are in trouble,
And when we have a meeting, you'll be out at the double!!"

"That's the end of me in here!" I thought. "What a bloomin' pity!
I've never been in trouble before, it's sad he's been so nitty.
I can't imagine all the mess, off a tiny packet of nuts,
Now I feel like a criminal, perhaps I should be in the stocks!!"

So take my lead and don't feed while you're playing snooker,
Rules and regulations have been passed, don't stick up your snooter,
Eating nuts is not allowed, because salt goes on your balls,
And if there's grease on the table, the balls won't go in the holes.

I didn't realise what I'd done was such a transgression.
If I'd thought it was that serious, I'd have popped into confession.
When you're out for enjoyment, watch how you chalk your cue,
Keep your nuts in your pockets, don't be tempted to chew.

Now I will swill my beer with good cheer in a nicer spot,
Where people have common sense, and their brains are more than a dot,
Where people can enjoy themselves, not be told, "You're acting the can,
And do as I say, but not as I do, because I'M A COMMITTEE MAN!!

THIS IS THE NIGHT

When the daylight closes its eyes, and the dark awakens to the sight of
a beautiful golden moon floating in a sea of a thousand twinkling stars,
This is the night.

Below a million street lights illuminate miles upon miles of highways
and byways, shining forth like beacons, guiding the restless travellers
home safely to their destinations -
This is the night.

In their homes people are preparing for rest, as the lights slowly
extinguish, and a pattern gradually forms over the landscape, like a
huge patchwork quilt -
This is the night.

An alley cat slowly makes his way over to a heap of plastic bags that
he hopes will yield something tasty, he unceremoniously claws them
open scattering the contents, adding to his already litter-strewn patch,
he meows his disgust at finding nothing, and then cocks his leg up and
piddles with scorn -
This is the night.

A fox emerges from the shadows, he has been watching the feline's
antics in a quiet bemused fashion and heads for the back of the heap;
after scavenging around, he came up with half a loaf of stale bread
which he quickly devoured, and then slunk quietly back into the
shadows -
This is the night.

An old man that's using a doorway as a bedroom, quietly adjusts the
rags that he's using for blankets, and pulls a sheet of polythene closer
to his body to keep out the biting wind -
This is the night.

A dog howls out his evening choral raptures, a voice cried out "shut
up", silence reigns for all of five minutes and then he starts up again,
followed by one or two other choir members -
This is the night.

A thief stealthily moves in the deep shadows carrying his stolen bounty, he stumbles and curses his ill-found luck as his swag scatters covering the ground, he picks himself up and hot foots it down the road

This is the night.

An ambulance winds its way through the streets with its alarm bells ringing and lights flashing, there had been an accident, a police car responding to an emergency burglary call ran over a male, who happened to be running in the middle of the road, in an area where the street lamps had been vandalised -
This is the night.

THIS COULD BE THE END!

This could be the end,
Well, this could be the finish,
Nothing lasts forever,
All things must diminish.

I have had a darned good run
And nothing's meant to last!
The time has come to rest a while
And let the hours pass.

My pencil's shorter than it was,
My rubber's worn down thin!
And people have even commented
"Throw them in the bin!"

My paper's getting pretty scarce,
My life's got shorter by the minute,
But it's hardly not surprising
Because I did put on a limit.

It's time for me to pack my bags,
I will just get up and go,
But I'll not do anything hasty,
I'll just move away real slow.

I know when I'm not wanted,
I can take a hint!
I feel like the bit in the middle
That's missing from the mint!!

Well, now I'm going from this place,
My work will be departed
But out there there's no one good enough
To finish what I've started, Ha!

Part II

POETRY ABOUT
LOVE AND LIFE

The world is just a great big stage
With man the main part of the act.
Life is such a serious thing
And that's a God-proven fact.

We all need a little humour,
A small lightness to our strife.
We all like a funny man to come along
And show to us a funny side of life.

~oOo~

I hope that you enjoy my poetry
It has taken me away from strife
And after I was made redundant
It has given me a new lease of life.

I have done many things in my lifetime
But poetry was never a part,
My love and life is for you to read,
Each verse comes straight from my heart

Just to be able to write what I'm thinking
And to give people a whole lot of pleasure
Means more to me that all the money on earth
Because my love of life is my greatest treasure!

MY FRIEND AND MY WIFE

Please always love me, never let us part,
Always be a part of me, next to my heart.
When I first met you I "knew" you were the one,
I want to spend my life with you, until my time has come.

You are all that I have prayed for, my true guiding light,
You are the woman that I cherish, my Venus in sight,
You make me feel so happy, when you are by my side,
You give to me contentment, and fill me full of pride.

Out of all of the millions of girls that are around
You are the only one I've chosen, the right girl that I've found.
I will never want to harm you, or to send you away,
I want you, darling, forever, my love always to stay.

You are so gentle and caring, all goodness and right,
You make my heart sing, and dance with delight,
I love you truly, and I want you to know
That you are always in my thoughts wherever I go.

You fill my heart, my whole body and soul,
You have taken me over, completely and whole,
You have given my life meaning, in all that I do,
And to make you feel happy, I will do anything for you.

If others had our happiness, they would never separate,
I can't understand why so many have heart-break.
When you've found the one you love, who is honest and true,
Then be happy together, and forget someone anew.

Cherish your partner, and they will do the same,
Love is eternal, please don't put out the flame,
Be happy together, we have only one life,
That is why my partner is my friend and my wife.

WALK WITH ME

Walk with me in the summertime, Love,
When the sun has warmed the land,
Together we will stroll the lanes
Holding each other's hand.

Walk with me through green meadows
Where the cowslip and buttercup meet,
And together we will dance through the daisies
As though we had wings on our feet.

Walk with me alongside a river bank,
We'll watch the water gently run to the sea,
And as light glistens on the shimmering water
We will follow it, as far as we can see.

Walk with me 'neath the boughs of tall trees
And together we will stroll in the shade,
We will listen to the sound of birds singing
And enjoy the sweet music that's made.

Walk with me on the moorland through heather
And down the hillside, where bracken grows tall,
There we can watch the flight of the curlew
And hear the sound as he shrieks out his call.

Walk with me through gardens of great beauty,
And share the perfume and admire the colours on display,
Together we will share these gifts of nature
And see how man has gently nurtured them his way.

Walk with me hand in hand through this life, dear,
So that I need never walk it alone,
Side by side we will walk it together
But please never leave me on my own!

EVEN THROUGH ETERNITY

When I hold you near me, dearest one,
My body trembles with desire,
And when I kiss your lips, my love,
I am consumed with a fire.

This passion I hold for you, dear heart,
Ignites just like a flame,
I want to tell you I love you, darling,
Over and over again!

When you are in my arms, dear one,
My heart beats with loving pleasure,
You are all that I yearn for, my sweetest love,
My very own priceless treasure.

Your hair is so lovely, my darling,
And your skin is so soft and fair,
To me you are just like an orchid, my love,
So fragrant and delicately rare.

God has chosen you for me, sweet love,
All for my very own,
I give to you my heart, dear one,
My whole body and soul.

You will always be a part of me
Because together we are one,
Nothing will ever separate us, dearest,
Until God's will is done!

The love that I hold for you, dear heart,
Is for everyone to see,
We will spend out lives together, my love,
Even through eternity!

I WILL HAVE TO STAND IN LINE

I knew you as a flower in bud
When first you caught my eye,
And then you'd bloomed into a rose
The next time I did espy.

Your vision swirled around my head,
My thoughts were overcome,
My body turned from hot to cold,
I have never felt so numb.

You truly are a beautiful sight,
The like I have never before seen,
And the way you float before my eyes
I could swear you are a dream.

I have known you since my childhood,
Only then you were a girl,
Now you have grown into a woman
And my head's begun to whirl.

I can't believe how much you've grown,
How life has moved so fast,
From a girl to a beautiful princess,
How time has quickly passed!

I'm the lad who knew you as a lass,
Now I want you for my own,
I just can't believe my feelings
Or the fact that you have grown.

I long to hold you in my arms
And say, "Will you be mine?"
But there's a queue outside your door
And so I will have to stand in line!

HER BEAUTY HOLDS MY SIGHT

Show to me a face of radiant beauty
With eyes that shine and sparkle in the light
And lips that are so soft warm and tender
For when I kiss them, and whisper good night!

Present to me the picture of an angel
That portrays to me a heart of pure gold,
And let her have a smile of glowing enchantment,
I want her to be a wonder to behold.

Mould for me a woman cast in bronze
And blend in faith and courage, like Helen of Troy!
Make this figure resplendent in all its glory,
And may all who look upon her fill with joy.

Shape for me in clay a woman who is regal,
And give to her the majesty of a Queen,
Let her have the refined elegance of a lady
With a naturalness that has never before been seen.

Sculpture me a woman out of marble
And give to her the form of pure grace,
Make her to have the figure of perfection
So all will want to look upon her face.

Let me see a vision of pure loveliness,
A woman with a body that's so fine,
And let all who see her cry out with admiration
And let anyone who touches her feel divine.

Now show to me a face of radiant beauty
With eyes that shine and twinkle in the light,
That's the face of my true love you have shown me,
And she's the only one who's beauty holds my sight!

WE CARE

What makes me want
To break down and cry?
What makes my heartache
And inwardly sigh?

What fills me with torment
And deep down despair?
I know it's the thought of you
Not always being there.

When I first set my eyes on you
At the age of sixteen,
From that very moment on
You have been my Queen.

It's a wonderful strange sensation
When love is in the air,
People say, "It isn't important,
And at your age you shouldn't care!"

You were turned seventeen
When I made you my bride,
Almost thirty five years have passed
And still you're my pride.

I cannot define love
But our bond is very rare,
Our secret is no secret,
We just show each other that we care!

LOVE

Love is such a beautiful word
And in essence it's a wonderful thing,
I want you to know that I love you so!
Oh, the joy and happiness those few words bring.

Love is a word for everyone.
A word so meaningful and rare,
And love is given with true affections
To show how much we really care.

"I love you!" will always be
The words that give our most pleasure,
The endearing of the sentiment
Is something that we will always treasure!

The way we demonstrate our love
Is shown in so many different ways,
It is lovely to give all life affection
And brings sunshine into their days.

The love that we share with our children
Or our father and our mother,
The love that we have for our sweetheart
Or our grandfather and grandmother.

The love that we share with animals
And all things here on earth,
The love we share with one another
And thank God for giving us birth.

Love is that extra special word
That comes straight from the heart,
I always want to share my love
Until I from this world depart!

TRUE LOVE

To have loved and lost in this world is sad,
But to have found love is a very rare treasure,
For to have caring and sharing in our lives
Must be the world's greatest pleasure.

Man was not born to live alone,
We are not meant to be separated,
God intended men and women to be as one
With a love that is not divided.

To share our love with someone else
Must be our greatest gift of all,
To find someone who will share our life
Until we hear God's call.

The happiness and joy we give
To another individual
Is an emotion that is returned tenfold,
Making us feel extra special.

It isn't difficult to give and take,
It's not hard to share with another,
Particularly if it's your chosen one,
The person who you'll love forever.

If we were meant to be alone,
The world would just cease living,
We would have no need for love and sharing,
And there would be no sense in giving.

But to hold onto what you have got,
And to show to them how much you treasure,
Is to let them see your love every day
Because in true love there is no measure!

MY WEDDING DAY

As I stand at the altar, waiting for my bride,
I have waited for this day, when she would be by my side,
My heart feels so enlightened, and I hear the wedding song,
Here comes the bride, to me she will soon belong.

People's heads turn, they are all wanting to see
This beautiful woman who's coming to join me,
I hear one or two gasps as she's held in their sight,
Looking at my intended, a true vision of delight.

Moments pass quickly, and then she's stood by my side
I glanced and I smile, whilst my heart beats with pride,
She pushes back her veil, and in her eyes I can see
Just how much love she hold there for me.

The vicar utters, "Dearly beloved, we are gathered here today!"
My bride holds so much beauty that I can't look away.
I can hear the questions asked, and I carefully reply,
And then from the background I heard a gentle sigh.

The vicar raised his voice: "If anyone can show just cause?"
An eternity seems to elapse, but only a moment of pause.
"Who gives this woman?" the vicar solemnly asked.
"I do!" stated her father, as he enjoyed the small task.

The vicar asks for the ring, it gets placed on the Book,
Nerves have affected the best man, his hand visibly shook.
"Do you take this woman, to have for your wife?"
I replied with sincerity, "She is my whole life!"

The ceremony was over, and I kissed my bride,
She is all I've ever wanted, all I've dreamed about inside.
Now time has flown by, and many years have gone past,
But we are still together, our love was meant to last.

MY LOVE FOR YOU

Your face is such a wondrous sight
And your beauty fills me with delight,
Your heart I hold with tender care
Whilst your love I cherish beyond compare.

The way you walk and the way you talk,
The way that you hold your knife and fork,
Your every mood and your every way
Is why I love you, every single day.

In heaven or on earth there is no light
That could ever shade you in my sight,
There has nothing as priceless ever been found,
In my life I have everything when you are around.

Whenever I hold you in my arms
I always feel your tender charms,
Your love, your warmth, your every passion
Is something for me that will always be in fashion.

I will always want you for my own
But I want you to know how my love has grown,
Just like a flower in the light
My love has blossomed overnight.

You are like a rose with a sweet perfume,
That's how the thought of you fills my room,
My heart, my soul, my every day,
I know that I would die, if you went away.

I always want you to be by my side,
My one and only beautiful bride,
In all that I say, and in all that I do
I can never show enough my love for you.

THIS MUST TRULY BY LOVE

When you came my way, dear,
Only you held the key
To open my heart, dear,
And set my love free.

You filled me with passion
And took away my very soul,
Now with my entire body
You own it all.

You have set me on fire,
Now I can't put out the flame,
My heart begins to smoulder
Whenever I hear your name.

In my dreams I revere you,
To my eyes you're my sight,
You are all that I live for,
My only shining light.

I always want you near me,
My dearest true love,
And when I gaze into your eyes
I'm sure you were sent from above!

Please don't ever leave me!
Never from my side depart,
Because if you should go, dear,
You take with you my heart.

What gives you this power over me?
Why can't I break free!
This must truly by love
That I hold for thee!

MY HEART BELONGS TO YOU

When I hold you in my arms
My heart begins to whirl,
I love you even more right now
Than when you were a girl.

You are the only one I've ever loved,
The only one who stood a chance,
I know that I'm the luckiest man,
You won me over with one glance.

Your smile is like the rising sun
So radiant and warm,
And when you utter sweet loving words
I'm overcome by your charm.

You will always be the one for me,
My love for you will never falter,
And as the months turn into years
My feelings will never alter.

We have shared in a lot of happiness
And sad times have been and gone,
Now when I hold you close to me
I feel nothing can ever go wrong.

When I've seen tears in your eyes
And sadness upon your face,
That's when I know why I fell in love,
No one could ever take your place.

You are the most wondrous person that I know
In everything you say and do,
That's why all the love that is in my heart
Belongs to only you!

I'M GOING TO TAKE YOUR HAND

Oh, my boat is waiting in the harbour
And soon I'll be sailing far away,
I am going to seek my fortune, love,
And then I'll come home to stay.

When I have sailed across the ocean
You will always be a part of my heart,
And the hardest thing that I will ever do
Is when I from you depart!

Please wait for me my dearest love,
Don't abandon me for someone new,
My heart will break if you forsake me
And I'll have nothing left to come home to.

When I return I'll build a house, sweet love,
A home that will be big and grand,
And I will furnish it with the very best, dear love,
We will have children and acres of land.

You will never want for anything again, my love,
I will give you all your heart desires,
And your gowns will be of the finest silks, dear heart,
Their beauty will set your heart on fire.

I will adorn you with priceless gems, sweetheart,
The like that has never before been seen,
And I will set you on a throne, oh dearest love,
Then you will be my beautiful queen.

So when I'm far away from you, my love,
Please remember all the things I have planned,
Then when I return, and all my promises are fulfilled,
I'm the man who's going to take your hand!

IN THE MISTY MOONLIGHT

In the misty moonlight
I sense your presence near,
And as you move towards me
I can see your beauty clear.

You look just like an angel,
Your face is graced by the evening light,
And your eyes they sparkle like diamonds
Under the pale moonlight.

You appear to float just like a cloud,
You hardly move your feet,
And I stand as thought I am in a trance,
Your form is so elite.

Your voice is like a gentle breeze
Slowly floating in the air,
And moonlight gives the softest glow
Like a halo around your hair.

Your touch is like an angel's breath
Gently wafting all around,
Your kiss has a taste like nectar,
The sweetest one I've found.

My head swirls just like a whirlpool
And my feet are treading air,
My heart beats with excitement,
I just can't believe you are there.

I take you gently in my arms,
My passion races with desire,
There's only you can put out this burning flame,
You're the only one who can extinguish the fire!!

MY LOVE WILL NEVER DIE

My love will never die for you,
You will always be my life,
My every dream I dream of you,
My ever loving wife.

My every breath I breathe for you,
My being is yours alone,
My sight and everything I see
Through your love I have been shown.

I hold your vision in my head
Each time that we are apart,
I never want you to leave my side,
You are always in my heart.

If there's anything I can do for you
Then all you have to do is ask,
Nothing could ever be a burden
And there's nothing that could be a task.

When I hold you in my arms, my love,
You are everything that I need,
No one could ever take your place,
You are my heart and soul indeed.

My love for you is everlasting,
Just like the heavens, so high in the sky,
I always want to be here for you,
My love will never fade nor die.

All I ask for is only you, my love,
All I want is just you alone,
To share this life with me, my love,
I want you to be mine for my own.

EVELYN

I could never stop loving you,
What more is there to say?
My heart would die, I know,
If ever you went away.

You are all that I live for,
You're my whole life through,
And if you should ever leave me
Than my world dies with you.

Men dream about great riches
Like vast fortunes untold,
But you are my greatest treasure
To have and to hold.

I will never ask for a kingdom
And I never want to be a king,
Because when you are in my arms, dear,
I know that I have everything.

The stars that shine in the darkness
Are a miracle from above,
And when I met you, my darling,
I found the miracle of love.

The world holds great beauties
And sights to behold,
But my love for you, dearest,
Is no secret that I can hold.

Now when I think about nature
And God's gift to us all,
Then I think about my Evelyn,
God' greatest gift to me of all!

EVEN IN THE NIGHT

Paint for me a landscape of mountains and trees,
Brush on a meadow with humming birds and bees,
Add in some colour, with flowers all around,
And frame it with sunlight, making its beauty resound.

Please paint for me a picture of a white turtle dove,
And paint me a portrait of the woman I love,
Brush on for me the beauty that I see every day,
And paint for me the smile that says "Never go away!"

Mix in some silver for the colour of her hair,
And use a soft gentle brush for her complexion so fair,
Paint in every line with the lightest of touch,
These are the signs that she has given so much.

Paint for me her eyes, and make them sparkling bright,
They drew me out of the darkness, and into the light,
Gently paint for me her face that is lovely and kind,
And paint for me her thoughts that bring goodness to mind.

Put her shape on the canvas, with soft gentle form,
Show off her contour, and heart that is warm,
Paint for me her legs, and put grace in her stance,
Please paint for me the woman I fell for with one glance.

Paint in her vivacity and soft subtle charm,
Brush in her temperament, that is gentle and calm,
Paint in understanding, and deep thoughtful ways,
Paint for me the woman I'll love, for the rest of my days.

Please paint for me a picture of the woman that I love,
And then everyone can wonder at my angel from above,
Please brush with soft strokes and surround her with light,
So nothing outshines her beauty, even in the night.

WE WANT TO LEAVE TOGETHER

Please take me with you when you go,
I don't want to be left behind,
We have walked together hand in hand,
Our love has been our bind.

We have shared this life through thick and thin,
And nought has come between us,
Our love remains just as strong today
As when the good Lord joined us.

Like most folk, we've had our ups and downs,
But that's just a part of living,
Yet we have always managed to set things right,
That's a part of our sharing and giving.

We have had our share of heartbreak,
But our love has held us together,
We have never felt the need for anyone else,
Because we have always had one another.

You have always given me happiness,
And you are my pride and joy,
I could never imagine life without you,
There would be nothing left for me to enjoy.

We have shared in so many lovely things,
Now our lives are just flying on by,
When I think we haven't much longer on this earth
I just look at you and want to cry.

So if the good Lord should say to you,
"The time has come for your final letter!"
Just write to him a few lines and say,
"Lord, we want to leave together!"

GOD WILL SHOW US HIS LOVE

When I entered this world, I thought people were unkind
Because no one said, "Welcome!" They just slapped my behind.
A little later on, my mother had me baptised,
And whilst that was happening, I got water in my eyes!

Further on in my life, I started going to school,
But it wasn't for me, I was always breaking some rule,
And if anything went wrong, it was always me they'd suspect.
Mind you, before I left they made me a prefect!"

And then in my teens, I met a girl who for me was right!
I thought her an angel, my life changed overnight.
I couldn't believe her beauty, and the goodness she held,
And when I took her out, my head wasn't half swelled!

Later on we were married and had kids numbering three,
Two boys and a girl, they made me proud as could be.
And then they grew up, married, and got themselves a home,
Then they moved away, leaving my wife and me alone.

Well, they come to visit, it's nice to see them now and then.
It's funny, when they were kids our lives were ruled by them.
Yes, we really love our kids, and it isn't just a show,
It's nice when they come visit, and sometimes nicer when they go!

Now as I've gotten older, I think about the chain of life,
Of how I was brought up, the trouble and the strife,
Will my kids be happy, or will their lives be tough?
Will someone smooth out their bumps, or will their road be rough!

There can only be on answer, be honest, good and kind,
And put your faith in God, to receive peace of mind,
Love your fellow man, and treat him as a brother,
Then God will show to us his love, for our loving one another.

WHAT IS LOVE?

It's a wonderful affection, for all who live on earth,
It's a gift sent down from God above, after he gave us birth,
It's something very precious, as precious as life itself,
No one can take it away from you, it's given by yourself.

It's the first embrace of a new born child, as you hold it in your arms,
It's all that we feel for others, who share with us their charms,
It's tenderness and understanding, for when we need to care,
It's being able to give consolation, if someone should need us there.

It's like a soft warm breeze in summer, gently wafting on your face,
No one can describe the wind, but you can feel it's soft embrace,
It's like walking in a meadow, and watching new-born lambs,
It's like standing in the moonlight, kissing a girl and holding hands.

It's an emotion, it's a feeling, it's like spring water on your face,
It's a tingling, an excitement, a sweet God-given grace,
It's being caring and compassionate, in everything we do,
It's just like running barefoot, in the early morning dew.

It's the tears that we shed for the helpless, the homeless and the blind,
It's the pain that we feel for the crippled, and the simple of mind,
It's the beautiful scent of honeysuckle and jasmine in the air,
Whatever it is, as long as there's life, love will always be there.

Love is one of the most precious gifts ever bestowed on man,
It's handed down from heaven, by God's almighty hand,
But it's a gift that has to be nurtured, it's an emotion that has to be shared,
And it can only be done by people, to show that they really care!

YOU WILL ALWAYS HAVE MY LOVE

When I see you in the garden
With moonlight shining on your hair,
Your vision hold me in enchantment
And my heart whispers that I care.

All the stars shine in the heavens,
High above they twinkle bright,
But nothing can outshine your beauty,
In this wondrous waxen light.

Your eyes look like pools of water
Shimmering silver, round and deep,
I can't imagine anything more lovely,
Just like an angel, being awoke from sleep.

You walk towards me like Aphrodite,
I can see the look of love on your face,
I feel overcome with a raging passion,
And I say to myself, "This is the place!"

My arms enfold you, as I crush you to me,
We kiss, and the stars join into one,
I hear singing, coming from above me,
The heavenly hosts are watching over us in song.

I can't explain my feelings about you,
You're the only woman who can set me aglow,
But I know that I love everything about you,
And I always will because my heart tells me so!

You are my heaven, my whole constellation,
You give to me life, and a reason to live,
Without you I'm nothing, just total darkness,
You will always have my love, as long as I have love to give.

THE TRAMP

As I walked along a country lane, a tramp I chanced to meet,
He was a figure of despair, and wore little on his feet,
His face looked gaunt and worn with age. His eyes looked tired and sad,
His back was bent and he limped along, of my company he was glad.

"Let us rest awhile!" I told him. "Don't let us waste this lovely day,
And tell me, pray, what caused your plight?" "It's sad, the least to say!
I was the captain of a sailing ship!" he said, as his eyes misted over,
"And I have sailed the seven seas. My ship was berthed at Dover.

One day I met a beautiful girl, she gave me a chance to court,
We fell in love and planned to wed, the next time I was in port.
I set my course and sailed away, to a far and distant land,
I bought her presents and a ring, for the wedding we had planned.

I sailed again, my heart was light, because I knew I was going home,
And I had made avow when we were wed, no longer would I roam.
The sea was now hell-bent in rage, I commanded 'put on more sail!'
Then the rain came down in torrents, as the wind began to wail.

The crew recoiled in terror, as I called out 'More of you aloft!'
The waves were crashing o'er the ship and the bulwark was troughed.
Lightning struck a topsail, men fell screaming at my feet,
But all I could see was the vision that I was sailing home to meet.

The ship floundered in the storm, and sank to a watery grave,
And out of a crew of two hundred, only ten men did I save.
We were cast away on an island, and for three long years confined,
Until we were finally rescued, and I sailed home, my loved one to find.

I returned to the place we had pledged our troth, to the place I had departed,
And found God had taken her to heaven above, and left me broken-hearted.
Now! I'm not looking for any pity, and I bid you a fond good day,
I have loved and lost at an awful cost, but she's waiting for me on my way!"

I'LL NEVER WALK ALONE

I wandered quietly alone by the lakeside,
Like a cloud gently floats beneath the sky,
My mood was one of deep contemplation,
With time just slowly passing me by.

I gazed over the silver shimmering water,
It was like a picture, so colourful and bright,
With a landscape laid out on a canvas
Framed with a beautiful golden light.

I watched a sailboat gently cut through the water,
And from its wake water lapped upon the shore
Like kittens licking cream from off a saucer,
Then it faded, and stillness was with me once more.

I saw circles form as rain fell upon the water
But I couldn't feel the rain upon my face,
In my heart I felt that something was missing
As though a part of me had fallen out of place.

I walked along as I listened to the silence
And saw mountains, with their peaks snowy white,
I walked under tall trees, and through their shadows
And on into the day's shining light.

My eyes fell upon a lady who was crying,
She had tears gently rolling down her cheeks,
I wanted to offer her my consolation
But my mouth couldn't form the words to speak.

She sobbed that her darling had gone and left her,
He had drowned in the water, cold and deep,
She cried that she was going out there to join him,
And then together they would finally sleep.

She carried a rose as she walked down to the shoreline,
Then took her coat off, and placed it at her feet,
And then she quickly walked into the water,
She then trod where the water ran deep.

I looked on in horror as the water embraced her,
I couldn't move, my feet were stuck to the ground.
The water swirled until over her head she was covered,
And then suddenly there was not even a sound!

In my heart I had a deep feeling of enlightenment,
And then a rose was gently placed into my hand.
My dearest beloved had finally found me
And together we walked away hand in hand.

THE OLD LADY

I was walking down a narrow path
When suddenly I chanced to meet
A little only lady with long grey hair
And nothing on her feet.

"Excuse me!" I quietly spoke to her,
"Is everything all right?"
Her feet were cut and badly swollen,
She really looked a sight.

She looked at me through weary eyes
And said, "Son, my heart is heavy!
My husband passed away last week
And friends I have not any!"

I carried her back to her humble home
And gently bathed her feet,
She was the sweetest little old lady
That ever I've had chance to meet.

She said, "My husband and I were inseparable!
We went everywhere together.
We didn't need other people's company
Because we always had each other."

I said, "That's no reason to wander out!
Especially without any shoes!"
She replied, "I just wanted to get away!
I feel I have nothing left to lose!"

I told her, "Life is such a precious gift!
It isn't meant to be thrown away,
Your husband had been a lucky man,
But our lives all must end some day!"

I added, "Now I'll not leave you on your own!
Because in me you have found a friend.
I'll make sure that you never feel lonely
And some time together we'll spend!"

I paid visits to the old lady frequently
And we often went for a walk,
It cost me nothing to make her feel happy,
All that she wanted was to quietly talk.

She spoke to me of times in her childhood,
Of the happiness that had been and gone,
She told me how she had met her husband,
And how her heart he had finally won!

I said, "Even though he is no longer with you,
He will never be that far away,
Because the love that you had for one another
Is a love that will never ever stray.

I visited her again the very next evening,
And in the armchair she peacefully lay,
Cradling the photo of her beloved husband,
The lovely old lady had quietly passed away!

SONIA

God bestowed to us a baby girl, on the ninth of May,
A beautiful little gurgling child, it was our lucky day.
Her eyes were bright, her skin was fair, and beauty did abound,
Other children scream and shout, but she hardly made a sound.

This tender infant held a smile for all who passed her way,
She was a happy bundle of joy, and always wanted to play.
She filled our hearts and home full of happiness and joy,
We wanted a baby girl because we already had two boys.

Her laughter just like music, gently floating on the air,
And when she started crawling, she never seemed to care.
She would roll around and bump her head, but never shed a tear,
Life for her was an adventure, and she never held a fear.

If she had been a flower, then a rose would be her bloom,
Like a rose so full of beauty, her face brought love into a room,
But if she threw a tantrum, then just like the rose's thorn
You would feel the hell-bent prickle of a woman's scorn!

We have watched her grow up from a child into a lady fair,
With those sparkling laughing eyes, and beautiful golden hair.
She holds a sweet compassion for people young and old,
And she loves all kinds of animals, with a heart that's solid gold.

Well, now we've had a wedding, and she'd taken a lad called Chris,
You can tell they love each other, it seems the nearest thing to bliss.
We wish them every happiness, and hope their life together's long,
Like a beautiful-worded ballad, or a soft romantic song.

But reminiscing on her childhood, when she was a babe in arms,
With a face so full of beauty, she would beguile you with her charms,
That tender infant who had a smile for all who came her way,
Those early years I remember well, as the precious of all days.

DAVID

We have a son called David
And he makes us feel so proud,
He has never been a show off
Or wore clothes that were loud.

He is a lovely individual
With a personality that glows
In truth, he loves everybody
And he really lets it show.

He has never been a worry,
Even when he was a boy,
He brought us lots of happiness
And made our hearts overflow with joy.

He is always thoughtful and considerate
And to others he shows respect,
He never leaves anybody out
Or treats them with neglect.

Now he isn't a boy any longer,
He has grown up into a man,
And he couldn't be a better person
Even if that had been our plan.

But now he has gone and left us,
He has taken himself a wife,
And she is such a lovely person
That she is bound to enrich his life.

So now we are doubly happy,
But sadly they live far away,
So it means that we don't get the chance
Of seeing them every day.

MY MOTHER

My mother has the face of an angel
With lines of love etched in her brow,
Each line for the caring she has shown me
And her tenderness that has brought me to now.

Her understanding and kindness of nature
And the soft gentle feel of her touch,
Her soft spoken words of encouragement
Are only a part of why I love her so much.

Although she's only tiny in stature,
To me she's a hundred feet tall,
They say that goodness only comes in little parcels,
Maybe that's why God has made her so small.

Her eyes sparkle like a million stars above me
And her smile is so warm, soft and bright,
Like candles that burn in the darkness
Giving forth a beautiful, soft glowing light.

Her hair is the colour of silver
And her heart has been carved out of gold,
To me no one could ever be more cherished
Than my mother who had me to hold.

She always told me off when I was naughty
And her wisdom made me see wrong from right,
Now that I'm a man I can truly thank her
For giving me goodness and might.

This woman is so kind, and infinitely gentle,
And her affection so delicately rare,
In my heart my love will never diminish
For my mother who gave me life and sweet tender care!

MY BROTHER JOSEPH

My brother Joseph is such a lovely man,
But he has only ever known sadness and pain.
Still I love him so, and I want him to know
That he is in my thoughts time and time again.

I remember when a lad, he did his best to be bad,
And he never would leave anything alone.
He got up to all kinds of things. Nothing would change his whims,
But I know that his heart wasn't made of stone!

And then as he grew up, this life made him tough,
We can all change, because nothing is planned,
And the city's a hard place for anyone to face,
So it's easy for things to get out of hand.

Then he saw the light, and began to change for the right,
He married and took a wife for his own.
But then things went wrong like a sad-sounding song,
And once again he found himself all alone.

His life had turned sour, like a slow-wilting flower
When the petals begin to wither and fall,
I think he knew in his heart that this was the start
Of a slide that led to Nowhere at all.

Then he took another wife, I guess he thought that his life
Had begun to spiral way up to the sky.
But then after a few years, again came the tears,
Because he realised it was all just a lie.

Yes, he's been through the mill, and I know he's been ill,
If only I could have been more by his side.
I have more love for this man, more than any brother can,
My brother Joe, I speak of his name with pride!

MARCELLA

We have a lot to thank our son for,
He has always given us lots of pride,
But the greatest thanks we can offer him
Is for the girl, that he took for his bride.

These two people share a happiness
That has been given to them in life,
And we hope that with God's mercy
No one will ever cause them strife.

For to share a life together
You need commitment, truth and love,
And when these ingredients have been blended
You have been blessed by God above.

When our son brought this lovely young woman
From far across the sea,
Our hearts were filled with happiness
When he said, "This is my bride to be!"

Beauty is in the eye of the beholder,
So many times this I've been told,
But not only do we see her as beautiful,
She also has a "A great big heart of gold!"

In these few words I just want to say
About the happiness she's brought into our life,
And she will always be our special person,
The girl our son took for his wife.

Although their home is far away,
Our hearts will always remain together,
And our love grows dearly by the day
For our special daughter-in-law Marcella!

CHRISTOPHER

This man our daughter married
Is a lovely friendly lad.
He likes the sound of rock bands
And fast cars bring out his fad.

He'll talk about almost anything
That tends to come his way,
He finds most things interesting
And he loves to have a say.

They make a lovely happy couple,
Our daughter and her Chris,
And if we were called to judge them
Then we would call it "Married Bliss"!

When we see the two of them together
We can see their love is strong,
And that's what couples need today,
Maybe why so many are going wrong?

Chris is a very hard worker
And he knows just what's required,
He isn't one for lying in bed
Or always moaning that he's tired.

The pair of them make a darned good team,
Neither one of them spoils the other,
They join together in give and take
And that way there's no bother.

They know exactly what they want,
And strive to leave behind the rest,
I know that Chris is the kind of lad
Who will always do his very best.

MY GRANDMA

My grandma held a wisdom just like Solomon,
She was kind, gentle and so full of grace,
She had a comforting word for everyone around her
And she always wore a smile on her face.

Her front door would always be open
And the kettle was never off the boil,
She always made everyone feel welcome
Even if she was in the middle of her toil.

Her home held the sweet scent of roses
And nothing ever looked out of place,
In her presence you felt loved and special
And you always got a comforting embrace.

I remember the tales of her childhood,
I would sit on the floor by her knee,
She would hold me entranced by her stories
Of when she was about the same age as me.

Her hands were all gnarled and wrinkled
But they had the tenderness of an angel's caress,
When she smiled, her eyes twinkled like stardust
And her face held the beauty of a princess.

My grandma was my very special person,
I was lucky to have found all this love.
Now in my heart, a part of me is missing
Because she now lives in heaven above.

MISTY

She was eleven weeks old when I bought her
And as white as the pure driven snow,
She had a face, with a beauty that would haunt you
And a love that we were privileged to know.

Earlier in life, one of our children
Had been alarmed by a dog that had strayed,
And so by bringing Misty into their life
This was going to be the answer I prayed.

My wife stated, "I'm not an animal lover!"
But when Misty appeared out of the cold
Her dislike turned to love and affection
An emotion that was returned a thousandfold.

I need never have held any reservations
For all the joy and happiness she brought,
Our home was filled with love for each other
And now a special love that she taught.

Her temperament was one of an angel,
Her mannerism you could take anywhere,
She was never selfish or demanding
And for all of us, she would always be there.

She not only brought to us companionship,
She didn't only bring to us love,
She brought to us a greater understanding
Of a different life, from God up above.

Now she is gone, she will never be forgotten,
In our thoughts she will always be there.
When a part of your life has sadly left you
There will always be a vacant chair

A LONELY COTTAGE

In the glade there stands a cottage
Dazzling white in the noonday sun,
It looks so beautiful and yet so lonely,
Built by a man for his beloved one.

They were betrothed to be married,
A handsome boy and a beautiful maid,
For he promised her this cottage
And he would build it in the glade.

He built the cottage before their wedding
And both of them were filled with glee,
But then came news of his father's dying
And his father lived far across the sea..

He sailed across the deep blue water,
Leaving his betrothed far behind,
But he told her before his ship sailed
That she would always be on his mind.

Love will cross a thousand oceans,
If it's true, then it's sure to last.
"I will soon return, and then we'll marry,
This to you I make my pact."

He didn't return, though she waited,
Then she received news that he had wed,
Across the sea he had met another,
And now she wished that she was dead!

She returned to where they had parted,
To where they had kissed so tenderly,
She looked into the deep blue water
And then threw herself into the sea.

In the glade there stands a cottage
Dazzling white in the noonday sun,
Waiting for a couple who were to be married
Built by a man for his beloved one.

IN A COTTAGE AT THE BOTTOM O' THE MOOR

We lived in a cottage, at the bottom o' the moor,
Beauty was in abundance, surrounding our door,
We had no modern refinements, electricity or gas,
Our water ran down the hillside, and along through the grass.

Our visitors were scarce, and people often not seen,
It held a charm of its own, with beauty serene.
Our mother worked hard, baking, washing, and sewing,
We didn't have fitted carpets, just a peg rug and cold flooring.

I don't remember wall coverings, just walls that were white,
An oil lamp hung from the ceiling, giving off a dimly lit light,
The winters were long, and the snow was so white,
When you came in from the cold, the fire embers burned bright.

We were only children, and our parents were poor,
Our treasure the gift of nature, on the side of the moor.
Life passed us by slowly, everything moved at a gentle pace,
When you dwell amongst nature, you have no reason to race.

We kept goats, geese, ducks, pigs and hens in a pen,
It was just like a menagerie, if I cast my mind back to then,
And wild animals would wander, without any fear
For they had plenty of cover, if danger should come near.

My father grew tobacco, vegetables and flowers,
He would toil in the garden, for many long hours,
And when he came inside, each one of us knew
Of the pride that he nurtured for the things that he grew.

Sometimes when it's peaceful, and I start to reflect
On the times of my childhood, another time in perspect,
I see a garden with the scent of roses, my mother stood by the door
Outside a small whitewashed cottage, at the bottom o' the moor.

AROSA

I was on holiday in Switzerland
Not too many years ago
When I chanced to visit a beautiful church
That was completely surrounded by snow.

It stood silently majestic on a mountainside
All alone, peaceful, and serene,
Tears filled my eyes with emotion,
It looked just like a wonderful dream.

The cemetery was cherished and cared for,
I have never before seen such delight,
There wasn't a sign of any animals
And not a trace of any vandalism in sight.

I walked over, and spoke to an old man
Who's wife was peacefully resting there.
He said, "This place is called Arosa!
And God treats it with special care."

The air I breathed was so fine and fresh
And the water so sparkling and clear,
I think I know why he happened to mention
About God being so near!

Out of all the places that I have visited
And all the sights that I have ever seen,
Arose brings to me wonderful memories
The like I have never before dreamed.

There's times I often think about the old man,
And his words always come to bare,
He said, "This place is called Arosa
And God treats it with special care."

ON THE SIDE OF A MOUNTAIN

On the side of a mountain
Sipping spring water from a stream,
Looking down on a village far below,

You can't describe the beauty
Or the feelings in your heart,
It's like something that you've read so long ago.

A stranger would be passing
And he'd call out, "Hello, my friend!"
As he continued on his journey up the slope.

Your heart would feel enlightened
And the time would pass so slow
As you call back, "Please be careful how you go!"

The birds would sing in tune
And the sun would shine so bright
On the snow-laden peaks that stretch up high,

And all would be at peace,
You would be alone with God,
With your arms outstretched you could almost touch the sky.

On the side of a mountain
Where the flowers dance with glee
And life holds a freedom of its own,

Nothing disturbs the silence,
Only the gentle whisper of the wind,
And your heart becomes a part of the beauty shown.

MY PRECIOUS HOME, SWEET HOME

I have scaled the heights of mountains
And sailed across many seas,
I have visited many a distant shore,
There's lots of places I've wanted to see.

But of all the sights that I have seen
And foreign lands that I have roamed,
There is no place that has suited me best
Than my precious home, sweet home.

I think about the small familiar garden
With roses around the door,
The beautiful scent of honeysuckle
That seems to linger forever more.

A robin with his breast of red
Seems always on the scene
And the ivy, as it twists and turns
With its different shades of green.

A picket fence shines gleaming white
In the glorious noonday sun,
And the tiny windows' dancing light
As sunbeams have their fun.

A pathway that leads you to a step
That's been gradually worn with time,
And a door that's old and weathered
With a welcome most sublime.

You will enter through the doorway
To a shining polished floor
As the scent of lavender greets you
And says "Welcome home once more!"

You walk around from room to room
As though you have never been away,
And everything around you says
"We hope that you are home to stay."

Your clothes are how you left them,
Neat and folded in the drawers,
Your shoes are clean and polished
All lined up on the floor.

The furniture wants dusting,
But there's nothing out of place,
It is just how you remember,
There's no palace could replace!

But I haven't done with roving
Although I would like to stay,
There's lots more that I want to see
Before I fade away.

But when I'm through with wandering
And I'm feeling too tired to roam,
Then this is where I'll end my days
In my precious home, sweet home.

AN UNSEEN HAND
In dedication to my friend Kathleen Pattinson

Oh! how the moon glistens o'er the mild-tempered sea,
And the boats gently ride upon the tide,
The wind holds its breath, and not a ripple can be seen,
Whilst the stars in the sky quietly bide.

The night is so silent, and the heavens remain still,
Nothing stirs in the sky up above,
Sometimes peace and tranquillity make wonders exist,
Like the sweet tender words of love.

The boats cast their shadows in the moon's golden path,
With their rigging just like cobwebs hanging high!
The stars gently twinkle, like tiny beacons overhead,
Whilst the sea meets the earth with a subtle sigh!

The tide just rolls along, like the beautiful lyrics of a song,
Whilst music's the gentle whisper of the wind,
Under the moon's steadfast gaze roves the passing of the waves,
Showing the freedom of the water, with nought to bind.

Across the water's silver sheen the moon's halo throws his beam,
Casting a golden pathway across the sea.
A million courses have been set, and some with regret,
By the souls who had a yearning to be free.

The waters rush to meet the ground beneath my feet,
Whilst the moon silhouettes the cliff tops high,
And nothing can be heard, not the sound of a bird,
All's silent on the earth and in the sky.

The moon light softly shows, the water's gentle flows,
As the tide makes it ripple along the sand.
The boats gently ride at anchor on the tide,
And everything is held in place, by an unseen hand.

THE PLACE THAT I BELONG
In dedication to my friend Marlene Hubbold

I wandered o'er a cliff top high, alone with only God and sky,
My thanks to heaven in its grace, for showing me to this lovely place.
The magnitude of beauty there, gives me guilt with loath to share,
My heart danced light with nature's song, this is the place that I belong.

I looked before me, and could not believe, the beauty God had chanced to weave,
Like in a dream its shape was there, woven with such loving care.
The harmony of colours bright, made this a truly heavenly sight,
Where flowers breathed the air so clean, and I took in this wondrous scene.

The fragrance from the earth did rise, like a vapour drifting to the skies,
Such is the fondness of my heart, I cannot from this place depart
Where birds, and butterflies, and flowers, while away the passing hours.
Peace and tranquillity is all that's found, standing on this hallowed ground.

New-found beauty is so rare, when everything around is bare,
Where light shines gently on the hilltop green, and ten thousand sights are seen.
This solitude, this peace of mind, has been passed down for me to find,
Where no one's passed this way before, and followed it through to God's front
door,

Where light and shade repose in rest, and beauty is in heaven blessed,
Where nothing harms the creatures small, and love and peace lay over all.
On this hilltop I have found, my peace with God and all around,
My heart danced light with nature's song, this is the place that I belong.

THE MOUNTAINS ARE CALLING

The mountains are calling, calling out to me,
Come home to your loved ones, home from the sea.
I sailed in a summer, now three years have gone by
And all that's in front of me, is the sea and the sky.

I love the mountains, with their peaks gleaming white,
And the glaciers that sparkle under the sun's shining light,
I love the wild flowers that grow on the rocks,
The grace of the birds, and the antelope flocks.

Nothing can equal those towers on high,
Like fingers from God, pointing up to the sky,
The air is so pure, and the water runs clean,
There's a feeling of contentment, and all sights to be seen.

I love those pinnacles, the rocks and the shale,
I respect the challenge, and the right to assail,
I drink from the water that falls from above,
And treat all the animals with sweet tender love.

That is why I miss those mountains so high,
And that's why I love those peaks in the sky.
Man can build forever, but never replace
My beautiful mountains of elegance and grace.

The mountains are calling, come home from the sea,
They echo across hilltops, and valleys to me,
My heart is aching, no more will I roam,
But I'll stay on in the mountains, near God's chosen home.

IN A BEAUTIFUL GLADE

The sun filters down through the treetops on high,
Highlighting soft patches of colour to my eye,
All shades of green are seen in the light
Like a jewel-filled casket, effulgence bright.

Shadows are cast in this serene woodland glade,
Peace and tranquillity is what God has made,
I've noticed a deer, quietly resting on the ground,
With a fawn by her side, not making a sound.

A squirrel scampered by, and ran up a tree,
He stopped, then peered back through the leaves, looking at me!
A blackbird called out from his nest up above,
Perhaps he is lonely? And wants someone to love!

Bluebells and primroses look pretty on the ground,
Making lovely patterns, with colour spread around,
Ivy clings to the trees in a tender embrace,
Whilst toadstools spring up, and gently show their face.

A butterfly flutters by, in a sunbeam's dancing light,
And a breeze, takes it through the trees out of sight,
A spider has quickly spun a fine silken web,
And then he's run into a corner, where he's waiting to be fed!

Nothing breaks the silence, there is stillness all around,
Only the sound of my feet, gently walking on the ground.
I can hear a pin drop, this quiet is so rare,
You'd think in the whole world, I was the only one there.

In this beautiful glade, I walk with sheet delight
And savour the moments, of nature's wonderful sight,
Amongst this serenity, I feel humble in this place,
Nothing in my imagination could be granted such grace.

I WILL NEVER UNDERSTAND

The waves gently lap and caress the rocks
And then fall back into the tide,
The spray rises up like a shower in the air
And sea-horses begin their ride.

The cliffs look weathered and worn away with age
Because storms have left them ravaged with time,
A seagull begins to take flight from his perch
And gracefully soars into a climb.

Algae stains the rock green far below
Whilst seaweed gets buffeted around,
Gulls fly in screaming as they come in to land
And the noise they made loudly resounds.

The sun gently breaks through the clouds high above
And a rainbow appears in the spray,
A sea-urchin moves with the flow of the tide
And then quietly gets washed away.

The waters foam white as they swirl around the rocks
And they sparkle in the sun's gentle beam,
A mist slowly lifts as though wanting to play,
And a haze makes it look like a dream.

A cloud moves across in the heavens above
And the sun no longer shines bright,
The scene becomes changed from a beautiful view
To one of shadows, each one wanting to fight.

The sea is no longer a beautiful green,
Instead its colours are now grey and black,
How nature can alter, with the sweep of a hand,
Is something that I will never understand.

ONE MORE STEP

I strolled along a path, on a cliff top high,
The stars were twinkling in the sky,
The moon was shining overhead
Lighting the pathway for my feet to tread.

The seagulls chorused nearby
Granting the night a lullaby,
Below me I could hear the sea
Washing o'er the rocks and breaking free.

A ship's horn broke the silent still
Awarding the night with an eerie chill,
Then sea mist gathered gently around
Concealing the pathway and the ground.

I stopped and looked up to the sky
And every star had closed its eye,
The moon no longer shone a light,
I felt like a man who had lost his sight.

I walked along, but held no fear,
For in my heart I knew God was near.
I believe that if you have faith
He will hold you in a fond embrace.

I still continued on my way
Then I held my breath, and began to pray.
Now I'm not a true God-fearing man
So I hoped for me "God had a plan"!

The mist began to fade away,
Then again the stars came out to play,
The light of the moon shone overhead,
One more step and I would have been dead!

SHE HAS NOT GOT A PRAYER

Several months ago she left these shores
And it was on a summer day,
The sky was blue and the wind was fair
When she quietly sailed away.

The skipper was a gallant man
Who had fought many a stormy sea,
And the good ship's name was the *Evelyn May*,
She had her mainsail billowing free.

Her course was set for the Americas
And her crew were hardy and bold,
They were taking supplies and passengers
To a land that was paved with gold:

To a land that was full of opportunity
Where milk and honey flowed free,
To where man didn't need to work at all,
He just planted a money tree.

Now on the ship sailed a cabin boy,
The youngsters name was Tom.
He said after he had finished on this passage
That he would be coming home!

Suddenly the sky began to darken
And the wind howled out a wail,
The waves began crashing upon the beach,
There was going to be a terrible gale.

We were stood waiting for the ship to sail in,
So that we could welcome our Tom home,
But now the sea was raging wild,
Maybe this would be him tomb.

The thunder-clouds roared overhead
As lightning lit up the day,
He told us that he loved us dearly,
Before he sailed away.

I heard a voice cry from behind me:
"No ship could last out there!!
No vessel could stay afloat in this,
She has not got a prayer!"

And now the wind was screaming,
The waves were mountainous high,
I slowly got down on my knees
And prayed, "Please god, don't let them die!"

All the people who were standing around me
Echoed loudly in my plea,
Suddenly the wind fell to a whisper
And a calm rippled over the sea.

Then out of the gloom appeared a shining light,
And someone called out, "There's a sail!!"
It was the good ship *Evelyn May,*
God had guided her through the gale!

LIVING OFF THE SEA

Where the sea and the sky come together
God gently nudges the night into day,
And as the sun faintly appears on the horizon
Seabirds herald the birth of a new day.

The fishing boats pull up their anchors
Now the tide's swiftly ebbing away,
And the wind fills their sails with laughter,
It's time to be getting under way.

They all put out to sea like an Armada,
Their sails glisten white in the sun,
Their aspirations are high for good weather
And a plentiful catch when they're done.

Their bows quickly break through the water
And leave a trail of white broken sea,
The fishing-grounds are now getting closer
And the nets are made ready to cast free.

They haul in their catch with enlightenment,
For today was a bountiful shoal,
Their spirits were high with expectation
Because tomorrow they may catch nothing at all!

When the men have done with their fishing
And back to this island they roam,
We wish them Godspeed on their journey
And a hazardless, safe passage home.

The sea holds a strange fascination
For the like of young boys and men,
But when you count on the sea for a living
It becomes a serious commitment then!!

SHIPSHAPE

I have always wanted to build a boat
And to sail both far and wide,
I wouldn't always use the sails,
I'd just drift along with the tide.

I would not plan a destination
Or even bother to chart a course,
I'd visit places that aren't on the map
Where people don't roam in force.

My craft would have lines sleek and trim
And would sail so fast and fleet,
Her sails would reach beyond the sky,
Only inches from God's feet

And when the ocean began to boil
I wouldn't make for a port,
Instead I would ride on the crests of waves
And listen to the wind's report.

The rain would lash down on my ship
And the deck would be awash,
But I'd still sail in that force ten gale,
And all my fears I would quash.

My boat would ride out any storm
And I would never be in danger,
For to pit its wit against the deep
My craft would be no stranger.

And when we finally reached calm water
I would anchor in a secluded bay,
And then I would gently lower her sails
And make her shipshape, for another day!

A BEAUTIFUL DREAM

I'm the Captain of a sailing ship, built out of peace and adoration
With clouds billowing with laughter for her sails,
Floating on a pool of endless sunshine, crewed by everyone I love,
Bound for a land where faith and hope prevail,

Guided on by shoals of dolphins, gently dancing on the waves,
Where their grace and beauty humbly outshine the sun,
Followed in our wake by every creature of the sea,
Knowing in their hearts, no harm to them will come.

We sail past islands filled with treasure, their beauty to enchant,
As waves softly lap the pure white glistening sand
And then float gently over coral, with its beauty held in mass,
As if sculptured by nature's tender loving hand.

We pass glaciers and icebergs, with cliffs reaching up on high
As if trying to stretch to heaven's open door,
A mist would gently enshroud us, as though wrapped in cotton wool,
And a soft warm breeze would hold us from the shore.

The stars would glitter bright, in the dark enclosed night,
And the ship would sail like a shadow, fine and trim,
Eight bells would sound and we'd all gather around,
To join the dolphins, in a beautiful moonlight swim.

And then with the morn, we would see a brand new dawn,
And watch the sun slowly rise from out of the sea,
And then our hearts will embrace God's bountiful grace
For giving us happiness, teaching us love, and keeping us free.

Then rainbows would appear, and embrace the land that grew near,
Like a jewel-encrusted crown it would seem,
And when we come ashore, I would awaken once more,
Because it was all just a beautiful dream.

MY ISLAND OF DREAMS

I dream of an island that's far out to sea,
Where the sun rarely sets, and the animals roam free,
Fruit grows in abundance, and the water's crystal clear,
And there's no sign of people ever coming near.

This is my island, my island of dreams,
My place of contentment, my home of esteems,
Where the wind only whispers, and the sea gurgles with mirth,
This is all that I've dreamed about, since the day of my birth.

I'll build a cottage from wood, with a roof thatched with reed,
And have a small garden, neatly planted with seed,
Then birds could come flocking, from all over the world,
And hold a banquet of good living, when my garden's unfurled.

I'll hitch up a hammock at the end of my plot,
In the shade of a palm tree, for when the sun gets too hot,
There'll be nothing to bother me, just long lazy days,
And there'll be no one to tell me, I've got to change my ways.

I can fish the blue water, and run along the sand,
I will enjoy my freedom, because nothing will be planned,
I'll climb the tall palm trees, and look out over the sea,
And watch the water gently break o'er the reef that surrounds me.

I'll stroll along the beach, with hardly a sound in the air,
Just the waves, gently lapping, and a bird here and there,
I'll stand and watch a turtle, with no haste to his stride,
As he walks from the sand, and gently swims with the tide.

This is my island, my island of dreams,
Where all that I hope for, a ray of sunshine that gleams,
A place of tranquillity, with sweet solitude and peace,
It's waiting for me out there, where slumbers never cease!

THE SEA

The sea gently murmurs as it ripples on the shore,
And the breeze gently wafts across the sand,
The seagulls' voices echo, as the sun starts going down,
And darkness gently falls upon the land.

The colour of the water changes from green, to murky black,
And the sunset mirrors on the gentle sea,
There's a feeling of contentment on the quiet sandy shore
As the tide allows the water to roll free

'Neath the waves fish are sleeping, though they never close their eyes,
And they gently move along, with the ebb and flow,
All life beneath the sea has quietly come to a rest,
And hardly anything moves on the ocean floor.

This vast expanse of water that covers most the land
Holds a mystery for me, as I'm standing here,
I can see the fascination as I gaze along the shore
For the seamen who sail out and show no fear.

When I think of all the lives the sea has taken through the years,
of the innocent people who've been lost and drowned,
My heart is filled with sadness, looking at the beauty that lays there,
Knowing it holds the secret of those lost and never found.

The sand-dunes stand aloof, like ghostly images on high
Sculptured by the wind and hands of passing time,
It's a moment of contemplation, as you gaze far out to sea,
And the water and the peace hold you sublime.

The sea holds many mysteries in its depths so cold and deep,
And for man it gives a calling to be free,
But whether man conquers the ocean, or the ocean conquers man,
Time and tide will give the answer about the sea!

GOD GAVE THE WORLD OCEANS

God gave to the world oceans,
The rivers and the seas,
And filled them with fish
To eat if we please.

He gave to us seabirds
And coral that forms a reef,
And he gave to us sand,
So we called it a beach.

We built ourselves boats
And discovered how to sail,
God threw in a few storms
And we called them a gale.

He put waves on the water
And introduced currents and tides,
Then he gave to us the courage
To sail the world wide.

When he gave to us these gifts
He would never have believed
That man could want to destroy
All the wonder that he'd conceived.

The oceans have become a rubbish dump,
We're polluting them with waste,
God gave to us these special gifts
But man's using them to debase!

We have lost all our respect for nature,
Everything's become grasping and greed!
But I think it's sad for the world tomorrow
When fish no longer breed.

THE MERMAID

It was early in the morning when I strolled along the beach,
And the sea mist gently floated o'er the sand,
That's when I heard a heavenly voice, gently riding on the breeze,
And I observed a mermaid, with a comb in her hand.

I quietly walked towards a boat that was leaning on its side,
And listened to her singing soft and sweet,
She slowly turned toward me and said, "Talk with me awhile!
Because with people I get little chance to meet."

I quickly walked to where she sat, she looked up at me and smiled.
I said, "You are the loveliest vision that I have ever seen!
No rarer sight, or purer sound, I have ever seen or heard,
I'm sure that God has sent me down a dream."

"We rest on the land every now and again," she murmured soft and low,
"But there isn't many of us left in the ocean deep.
Man is using the waters as a tipping ground, and he's killing off the sea,
It's very rare we sing, we mostly weep!"

"I wish that I was more than a man," I said, shaking my head.
"Everything that we touch, just ends up dying.
We don't seem to have respect for either land or sea,
And of that I feel sure there's no denying."

"I had two sisters!" she faintly sobbed, as a tear ran down her cheek.
"And now they've gone, I'm on my own, that's why it's nice to speak.
Where I come from it's beautiful, a kingdom beneath the sea,
But soon it will be barren, with nothing left for me."

I wiped the tears from her eyes, and gently kissed her cheek,
And then in the water I took her hand, and she led me out to sea.
Now if I don't die from pollution or radioactivity,
Then I'm probably on the sea bed drowned, *because I can't swim you
see!!*

THROUGH THE EYES OF A POET

Poetry is my greatest passion,
My works inspired by all I see,
This life for me is my education,
It's a tuition that is given out free.

Life's experiences makes me wonder,
What gives man the right to rule this world?
Could it be God's proven blunder?
And soon his wrath will be unfurled.

This planet has everything man could want for,
There's no need for greed or hostility.
What drives him on to total destruction?
I think his head's full of stupidity.

When you look around at what's on offer,
Just like a trader, who sets out his stall,
The air we breathe doesn't cost a penny
And there's plenty here, for one and all!

The earth itself is hardly ending
And all we need is a handful of seed,
When it rains, water's freely given,
Enough to satisfy all man's needs.

Trees and plants grew in abundance,
Animals roamed without fear or dread,
That's how it was before man's interference,
Now things are mostly dying or dead!

To put things right we need a miracle,
Maybe God's lost his faith in Man,
I see these things through the eyes of a poet,
And if I can see them, then others can!!

TO ALL WHO GIVE THEIR LOVE

What inspired me to pen this poem?
What gave me the urge to write?
I look at life through the eyes of Man,
It's not a very pleasant sight!

There's people begging on the streets,
The homeless and the poor,
And all they ask is for a crust of bread
And a key to a front door.

These people are only human beings,
Like us they are children of God,
They shouldn't be treated as garbage
Or something that's been left by a dog!

People talk about Christianity
And say, "Share and share alike!"
But I don't see a lot of action
From them with all the might!

The country's run on charity,
It's the poor giving to the poor,
You see, the well-off don't like it
When we knock on their front door!

I'm hearing about folk taking drugs
Or even committing suicide!
I only hope that things get better
When I am on the other side.

Now I know that I'm not the best of men!
But I help people when I can,
I would never dream of kicking a dog
Or causing any harm to Man.

In all my life I have never seen
So much jealousy and greed,
And that many people around me
Having so much more than they need!

I have never been a jealous person,
I just like to see people get on,
But not at the expense of others
Or just using life as a con!

The people who give their help to the needy
To me are saints indeed!
They prove that all people are not selfish
And the world does not revolve on greed!

Some day perhaps this world will change
But it will not be in my time!
I only hope that it changes for the better
And gets rid of all the slime!

So today I dedicate this verse,
It's for all who give their love,
And I hope they find their just reward
In the arms of God above!

THE SOCIETY OF THE NINETIES

I'm sick to death of the society that we live in.
Our fathers gave their lives for me and you.
They died to give us a better world tomorrow,
But their dreams for us just have not come true.

It's now the law of the gun, or the drug dealers,
Or the man who carries a knife, to feel brave.
It's a sign of the times that we live in,
I pray to the Lord our souls to save!

The law seems to side with the criminal,
The victim serves life for being true.
It's always the innocents that suffer,
Now the honest and upright are becoming few!

An eye for an eye is my answer,
Let's make the punishment fit the crime!
When life has been given as the sentence
Let ninety-nine years be the time!

They say that we have the technology,
It's a sign of the nineties, that's true.
But what switch do we turn, or knob do we pull
To get rid of this rotten evil few?

We're heading straight into the Millennium,
A coming time of one thousand years,
I hope to God the future gets better,
Because I'm tired of all the weeping and tears.

If Man could only see what he's doing to others,
And not be selfish, greedy, grasping and all,
Then people could share in a better way of living
Instead of making it just a free for all!

TAKING WAYS!

There's a lot of folk who are going around stealing!
They certainly have many taking ways.
What makes people act so light-fingered?
Does it mean that crime really pays?

When I was young, people had very little,
But they never stole to make up their shortfall.
Not all of them had jobs and were working
And most of them didn't collect any dole.

It seems a lot of people today just aren't satisfied.
I think the more that they get, the more they want.
Maybe it has something to do with technology,
But there's some things even computers can't grant.

Motor cars have always seemed a prime target,
Maybe they're too easy to drive away.
But they're not only stolen for their value,
They're used for joy-riding through the streets in all day!

Shops, houses and churches have all been burgled
And people are getting mugged in the street.
It's like a replay of Oliver Twist and the Artful Dodger,
Thank God not everybody's brought up a tea leaf!

And if there's nothing worth taking, they wreak havoc,
They destroy and despoil all in sight.
What a pleasure these idiots get out of destruction,
It certainly is a sick way of achieving delight!!

THE TOWN WHERE I LIVE

I come from a town in the North West,
A ship-building town of old,
Where men worked with a pride and a passion
And inspiration was part of their soul.

Now it's just part of a memory,
But memories don't die, they just fade.
Maybe in time it will leave us
For a precedence has been set out and laid.

If only we could turn back the pages,
If our lives were in volumes of verse,
We could hide a lot of the heartache,
When in truth life is just the reverse.

In the past it was a town of prosperity,
And in the area there was work for one and all.
But now all we have is despondency
With a lot of young men on the dole!

It's sad to see people down-trodden
When you remember good times, and not the bad,
And people had money in their pockets
When employment was plenty to be had.

But nothing ever stays the same forever
And something has to give in its wake,
Being out of work is part of the circle
and a big piece of the heartbreak.

God didn't give men hands just to pray with,
He also meant for us to earn our bread,
If there's nothing on his earth that's worth living for,
Then we might just as well all be dead!

THE STREETS OF SHAME

Please give me your hand, to help me along,
I don't have a job, and my life's going wrong,
My wife has left me and has taken the kids,
I'm losing the house, and I'll soon be in digs.

No one will listen, they pretend to you they care,
And once your money's gone, no one's left there.
I'll soon be evicted, pretty soon I'll have nowt,
Please lend me your hand, to help pull me out.

You work all your life, for a roof over your head,
But at the end of the day, the sky's there instead.
The politicians all say, "We've never had it so good!"
I think they're all blind, and their heads made of wood.

I'm not on my own, there's thousands like me,
With nothing to look forward to, and no future to see.
Where do you go to, and to whom do you turn
When your life's a cesspool, with no wages to earn?

I'm not looking for charity, or anything that's free,
I don't want handouts, just a life that's due me.
I've paid my taxes, and I've never been in debt,
I'm not a bad person, and I share most I get.

I feel my life is over, even before it's begun,
Maybe I should be in a war, and get shot with a gun!
I'm not a criminal, but I'm being treated as such,
If I was a cripple, I would be provided with a crutch.

God give me strength, and others like me,
To ride out this storm of wretched poverty.
We are all born equal, under the skin we're the same,
So why do some live in mansions, while others walk the streets of shame?

149

BEFORE WE ARE OUT OF DATE

I seem to be forever chasing rainbows,
Perhaps my aspirations are too high.
Maybe I should try for something smaller
And be satisfied with that before I die!

Life appears to hold complications,
Barriers seem to go up overnight,
Everyone wants to throw in a big spanner
And say, "You want to get on. What's your right?"

Age becomes a stumbling-block for employment,
Especially if you're getting past your prime.
Age used to go hand in hand with experience,
But now I'm told I should be waiting for my time!

There's too many people holding fancy titles,
And the salaries they get are way too high.
The ordinary man isn't chasing after millions,
Just a decent wage to earn before he dies!

In my life I've seen so many disappointments,
When a man tries hard to find what isn't there.
We all strive to reach the end of the rainbow,
But all we find there buried is despair!

Still, we don't give up, that's not in our nature,
Some place else there lies that crock of gold.
As long as we don't die, we'll go on searching,
But the only thing that's found is we've grown old!

Life almost seems and endless struggle,
If I'm not fighting people, I'm fighting fate,
When all that I want is a decent living,
That's all anyone asks before we are out of date!

ONE OF THOSE FACES MIGHT BE YOU!

I am trying to find myself a job, but things don't look too bright,
I've wandered around from town to town, but still can't see the light.
I have read up all the papers, but they have nothing much to say,
I can't remember, as truth will have it, the last time I had some pay.

I'm getting older by the hour, instead of older by the day,
And when I walk into the job centre, nothing comes my way.
There's lines of faceless people, to see if anything's on offer,
But there's nothing there to tempt them, to bring cash in to their coffer.

I'm told, "You're over-educated!" or "You don't have enough sense!"
How many brains do you need to receive a little recompense?
If I had brains coming out of my ears, I couldn't work any harder.
And if I were a brain surgeon, I'd probably make a useless gardener.

The whole country's upside down, with young men walking the street.
All they ask for is employment, just enough to make ends meet.
I have never seen so many firms close their doors and bite the dust,
And all that men are shouting for is to earn an honest crust!

We aren't looking for any handouts, or words of sympathy,
We're not jealous of what others have, we don't want anything that's free.
We just want to earn a living, and put some pride back in our life,
Instead of walking around in circles, and tramping away our lives.

Well, tomorrow comes, tomorrow goes, tomorrow's another day,
And with luck a door will open, and once again I'll pay my way.
But until then all I see is faceless people in a queue,
So don't you think about tomorrow, because one of those faces might be you.

151

I COULD GET ALONG ON JUST RICE!

Money is the root of all evil,
That's what some people say!
Now wouldn't chance be a fine thing?
I've just enough to pay my way!

Mind, what I have had, I've never wasted,
But we all make silly mistakes,
I remember buying a boat once
And then wished I'd jumped into the lake!

I've never thought about being wealthy,
Wealth to me means a happy life!
Too many folks have lots of money
And all it's brought them is trouble and strife.

When people have priceless treasures,
All they do is to lock them away.
I don't see the point in all the hoarding
Because they never see the light of day!

When people say to me, "I've got plenty of money!"
I guess their trying to make me impressed,
But while I'm listening to all their bragging
All it does is to make me awfully depressed!!

I've never thought about living in a castle
Or a house that's surrounded by a moat.
I like my visitors to be nice caring people,
The rest of them just get on my goat!

No, wealth to me isn't all that important
As long as the people who are around me are nice.
If only I could survive without money,
Then I reckon I could get along on just rice!

I HAVE NEVER MADE A PLAN!

Another day is over, that's another day that's past,
My life is getting shorter, I don't think it's going to last.
I have seen so many things, some good, not all bad,
And one or two disasters that have made me feel truly sad.

But I must not grumble, I've been luckier than most.
Mind, I've never won a lot of money, or been first past the post.
I've met some really nice people, but there again some funny folk!
There's some who never utter a word, whilst others talk and talk.

I find that life's just like a book, each page is a different story,
My life's been quite eventful, but I've never found the glory.
I have always been a worker, and battled to get on,
I've never walked over people, my achievements are my own!

I have come across many characters, very few have left me bored,
I've turned my hand to many a task, but never gone overboard.
I have always finished what I'd started, nothing left half done,
In case I'm not around tomorrow my time has suddenly come!

But planning for tomorrow, well, I could never see the fun,
My life's been in the hands of fate, and I hoped for a decent run.
I have never really been let down, perhaps a little stumble,
But I've always got back up again, and had a quiet grumble.

The people I've had around me, I have always found to be good,
One or two a little strange, but we can't all be understood,
And my friends if I should need them, have all been staunch and true,
I would certainly repay their kindness, if my help was needed too.

I've been around for quite a bit, but not as long as some,
The path I've walked had a stone or two, it hasn't all been fun.
But all in all my life's been good, I have been a lucky man!
I put it down to fate because I have never made a plan!!

WISHES HOPES AND DREAMS

Wishes are the ideals that we hope for,
Aspirations or dreams to come true,
We all pray for a better world to live in
Or for something that won't make us feel blue.

We all ask for a better standard of living,
We all dream about a fortune or two,
We've all pulled a wishbone, or wished on a star,
For something that's special and new.

We all want for the weather to get better,
We all hope for the sky a beautiful hue,
We all wish to find love and understanding
From people who are honest and true.

In my dreams, I ride on the backs of winged horses,
And I ride away to a land that's all good,
There are no poor, infirm or old people,
And no one has to go without food.

Without a little hope and expectation
Our lives would be dreary and mundane.
They bring to us a small ray of sunshine,
Though tomorrow will still remain the same.

Wishes are hopes that we long for,
Our life is the reality of it all,
But without our dreams and aspirations
Life would mean nothing at all!

WHEN IT'S TIME FOR BED

When all the stars are out at night
And when the moon is shining bright,
When all is still and not a sound
And all are rested on the ground.

Now we find the time to dream,
Our mind brings visions to the scene,
We drift off to a faraway place
Where no one can harm us, and all is safe.

Our fantasies now begin to form
And in our head strange sights are born,
Some people dream of finding treasure,
Maybe it brings to them most pleasure.

There's folk who dream about winning money
But when they awaken, they don't find it funny!
Some people dream about what they would like to do,
But as yet their dreams have not come true!

Some people's dreams brings to them delight
Whilst others they find are a terrible sight.
Now dreams are meaningful, so some people say,
Yet when we awaken, they all go away!

I see people I love, sometimes from my past,
It's sad that my dreams aren't meant to last,
I dream of great times that have gone by
And I often awaken with a low gentle sigh.

In my dreams I imagine that I'm whisked away,
And sometimes I think that I would like to stay,
But dreams are nice visions, that float inside our head,
And we are only allowed them when it's time for bed!

I DREAM

I dream of a world that's filled with sunshine,
Where men give one another a hand
And everyone is treated as an equal,
Where no man wants every piece of land.

I dream about a world with no fighting,
Where peace and tranquillity reign,
A place that has no need for doctors
Because no one has sickness or pain.

I dream of a time of contentment,
When everyone is happy with their lot.
They're not bothered about the grass being greener
Or that someone has a much larger plot.

I dream about a world that's filled with giving,
Where happiness and pleasure abound,
A world that has no room for cheats or liars,
A world where honesty and trust is all around.

I dream of children only knowing joy and laughter,
With their hearts overflowing with love,
Without ever knowing the fear of danger,
And each child would hold the gentleness of a dove.

My dreams are about people loving people
And not looking away when someone's in need,
My dreams are about people, walking hand in hand
And forgetting about killing and greed!

IT'S A MIRACLE

Who created this earth, and made the sun in the sky,
And put stars in the heavens to twinkle on high?
Who gave us the oceans, with their water so deep,
And created the mountain, with its towering peak?

Who breathed into us life, with a will to go on,
And put birds in the sky, and taught them their song?
Who planted the trees, so they'd have a place to rest,
And gave to them knowledge on how to build their nest?

Who made it rain, sunshine and snow,
And gave us the seasons, for all things to grow?
Who was it put animals to roam on this earth,
And bestowed on them nature, to make love and give birth?

Who planted the grass, and made flowers bloom and grow,
And gave to us deserts, where no waters flow?
Who gave life to insects and put them on this earth,
And gave colour to butterflies on the day of their birth?

Who brings the wind, to blow up a storm,
Or the breeze that wafts faintly, gentle and warm?
Who makes the thunder and clouds want to fight,
And then brings out the lightning, to brighten up the night?

Who gave to us day, and then took away the light,
And in the darkness, someone called it night?
Who created this planet, and let woman give birth,
To me it's a miracle, the greatest miracle on earth?

IS HEAVEN WHERE I'M BOUND FOR?

Is heaven where I'm bound for?
Or is it the other place!?
Will I be given a halo?
Or handed a shovel in its place!?

We all aspire to get somewhere,
Albeit good or bad!
They say there's a place for angels
And the other's a place that is sad.

I can't say that I've been really wicked!
But I could have been a whole lot better.
I've gone my own way in a lot of things,
I have never really stuck to the letter!

But I have never been a selfish man,
I have never wanted what's not mine!
I've just got on with what I'm doing,
What other folk have is fine!

I like to think that I'm sociable
And get on with people and class,
But the folk I can't stand are the big heads
And the people who brag about brass!

Maybe we should make no exceptions
And everyone should be treated the same.
Just because some people have a weakness,
It doesn't give us the right to call "shame!"

But I'm not expecting any special treatment
When I pop my clogs and depart,
I'll just leave it up to the Almighty
And see if he hands me a shovel or a harp!!

MAY I PLEASE GO TO HEAVEN

When I die may I please go to heaven
And walk on the clouds up above,
I could play with the angels in God's garden
And share in their heavenly love.

I could bathe in the pools of endless sunshine
And count rainbows with their colours so gay,
I could make each star in the sky into a twinkle in my eye
And I would slide along the Milky Way.

I could paint the sky blue for the summertime
And colour it black for the night,
I would then add some grey, and bring clouds into play,
And watch the thunder and lightning fight.

When I die may I please go to heaven
And meet with my friends in the sky,
I miss them so much I guess we've kind of lost touch,
It would have been nice if we could have said good bye.

We could chat about the times we shared together,
And the good times, the happy and the sad,
And perhaps reflect on the joys of our childhood,
Maybe their life on this earth wasn't that bad.

Mind you, I wish that I'd been a better person,
More tolerant, understanding and all,
But you can't change what's done, of this life we have one,
So I pray to the Lord for my soul.

If I'm lucky and should be chosen for heaven,
I will thank God, for not passing me by,
Then I would join the heavenly hosts as an angel
And walk with pride, in my heaven in the sky.

I'M ONLY ME

I believe that there's somebody up there
But I don't believe he's watching over me.
Maybe it's because I'm not very important
And after all's said and done I'm only me!

I think that he must have his hands full
Because Man keeps him forever on his toes,
And when people say, "I'm a true believer!"
I say to myself, "God only knows!"

On this planet we have a mixture of people,
And not all of them make out to be good.
When they arrive for their final assessment,
Will God say they were simply misunderstood?

I like to take people as I find them,
There's a lot of folk have a good heart,
But not all of them believe in Jesus,
Still, that's no reason to set them apart!

Most of us need someone to believe it,
Though there's a lot who believe in riches and greed!
Me, I just pray for a better world tomorrow
Because nice people are all the riches I need!

I've heard it said this is our heaven we're living in!
And when we die, all we do is turn to dust.
Maybe it is our final endeavour,
But I still believe, in God I'll put my trust!

Yes, I do believe that somebody's up there,
And if he finds a moment to spare
Maybe he could glance in my direction,
I'm only me, but I'd still like to show him I care!!

LORD, WE CAN'T LIVE WITHOUT YOU!

My darling, if you should ever leave me
Then my life on this earth is through.
I would have no need for further tomorrows,
I just could not live without you!

My whole body would be empty,
You would leave behind a shell.
They say that time heals many things,
But a broken heart won't get well.

When we first came together
Under God's watchful eye,
I knew you were the one for me
When my heart gave out a sigh!

We have built our lives together
On a foundation of love and trust,
And our home is filled with happiness
With lots of laughter as a must.

We have had three lovely children,
A canary and a dog,
Sadly the dog died, and the kids moved away,
Now there is only you, me and God!

My life could never be more contented,
In everything I do it shows.
I thank the Lord for giving you life,
My cup certainly overflows!

If I had my life to live over
And God asked me, what would I do?
I would say, "Please give me the woman I love!
And, Lord, we cannot live without you!!"

THE FRIENDS THAT WE LOVE
In dedication to Derek, Lizabeth and Family

Heaven's door is never bolted
And the admission is given free,
All that's asked for is a caring heart
And a love for you and me.

In this world we meet many people
And the nice ones stay in our mind,
Love for people is a natural affection
And it proves our hearts are kind.

When you've grown up with somebody
And you were the best of friends,
I can't for the life of me see a reason
For why that friendship should ever end!

Though our lives become separated
And we all change, that's life, you see!
Each man's road has a different surface
That's all laid out in our destiny.

We may marry and have a family
Giving ourselves a deeper love,
Our circle of endearment begins to widen,
Even taking in God above.

Though our meeting has become less frequent
Our height in friendship has never fell,
And now our lives have been given more meaning
Because now we can love each other's family as well.

Although we may not be together
Our thoughts are with your family and you,
And when the Lord says it's time for parting
Our hearts will whisper, "A fond adieu!"

162

THANK YOU FOR YOUR FRIENDSHIP

*This poem is dedicated to my best friend and confidant
William Whidborne*

Thank you for your friendship,
Thanks for being my best friend,
You are always there when I need you,
We will be comrades to the end.

We have shared in some good times together.
Happy, sad, tears and all,
I am writing this poem with sincerity
Because, sincerely, you're my best friend of all.

We have had our differences between us
But nothing that could be taken to heart,
You have never been spiteful or jealous
Or done anything to break us apart.

You're someone to talk to when I'm in trouble,
You're someone to moan at when I'm upset,
You always give me reassuring answers
And help me to keep my temper in check.

It's comradeship that makes life worth living,
It's friendship that makes life the best,
I don't reckon that we're going to live forever,
If we did, forever for us wouldn't be a test.

On this earth we meet many people,
There's the good honest folk and the rest,
But when we came together in friendship
I reckon God picked out for me the very best!

NOT ALL ANGELS LIVE IN HEAVEN

People say they've never seen God or angels!
But I see angels every day,
There's the nurses, who look after the sick and dying,
And carers, who show compassion in a different way.

The volunteers who do endless work for charity
And don't expect any just reward,
There's the people who visit our hospitals
To keep some patients from feeling ignored,

The kind-hearted, who look in on old people,
And take them out, just to show them they care,
The people who pay calls on our prisons
To let the prisoners know that someone's out there.

Angels are around every corner,
People with love and a heart to bare!
And these people aren't after big hand-outs,
Their reward is in the love they all share!

What would we do without these angels?
Society would surely crumble apart.
Not everyone has a kind and loving nature,
It isn't everyone who can share with you their heart!

To me anyone who helps another is an angel
It's a person who gives love free, with no demand,
And they would give you their last penny, if they had one,
And their kindness comes from someone who understands.

No, I don't need to look hard to find angels,
I think they walk in the footsteps of God,
So if you're looking for our father who's in heaven,
Just tread where these angels have surely trod!

THERE BUT FOR THE GRACE OF GOD GO I

It's so sad to see the sick and the ailing
And to know that young people are going to die,
When I see youngsters with their heads clean-shaven
It makes me want to just break down and cry!

When I see people sitting alone in wheelchairs
They rarely have an expression on their face,
Their world is almost one of total confinement,
I wonder why God left them, out of place?

The blind live in a world of total darkness,
They can't see the difference between day and night,
They'll never see the sunshine from the heavens,
Or distinguish colour in the day's golden light!

There's the simple of mind, and the Mongols,
My list just doesn't seem to have an end,
With all the suffering and pain I see around me
My heart's broken, with no way for it to mend!

I can't believe, with all Man's ingenuity and wisdom,
That we seem to be going nowhere pretty fast!
Well now Man's reproductive genes are getting shorter,
So I think he hasn't that much longer, before he's past!

But for our time that remains on this planet
It would be nice if man would give more help to his fellowman!
Never mind saying that I'm doing alright, Jack,
And you make out the best that you can!!

More people on this earth should count their blessings
Because they aren't going to prematurely die,
And when they see the crippled, the sick, and the dying
They should say, "There but for the grace of God go I!"

I WOULD LIKE TO SEE THE SKY

I can't see the sunshine,
My world is the night,
But I can hear children's laughter
In my world without sight.

I can hear the birds singing
And feel the softness of the rain,
I know about loving
And sometimes the pain.

In my mind I see beauty
And wonderful things,
I can hear a bright orchestra
With soft gentle strings.

I can smell beautiful flowers
With petals soft as my face!
I can imagine their colours
And God-given grace

I can feel a light breeze
As it blows through my hair,
And I can walk in the shadows
Without even a care.

I can walk on the beach
And then, what is more,
I can run through the waves
As they wash o'er the shore.

My ears are my sight,
I'm just the same as you,
But I would like to see the sky
Before my days are through.

ISN'T THAT A SHAME?

I cannot hear and I cannot talk,
But I can see and I can walk,
I can read lips or see into your eyes,
And I can see light and the wonder of the skies.

I can't hear the rain as it falls all around,
But I can feel water, as it flows over the ground,
I can see the birds, as they fly through the sky,
But I can't hear them singing, and that causes me to sigh!

I can see flowers and smell perfumes so rare,
I can see kindness and sweet loving care,
I can feel tenderness and return your embrace,
And I can feel tears as they run down your face.

I can't hear the wind, as it howls through the trees,
And I can't hear the thunder as it roars on its knees,
But I can see the lightning as it lights up the earth,
And I can thank God for giving me my birth.

I can see children laughing at play,
And I know what they're thinking, without having to say!
I can see a storm without hearing its might,
And I can see trouble, with no sound from a fight!

I can't hear music, or notes that resound,
But I can tell from your face, it's a beautiful sound,
The language of animals falls on deaf ears,
But I can sense danger, and it fills me with fear!

I can give affection and offer you my heart,
I could offer you my world, but it's been yours from the start!
I can give you everything, and never ask for gain
But I can't hear you say, "I love you!" Isn't that a shame?

GOD MOVES IN MYSTERIOUS WAYS

As I was walking past a graveyard
I heard a gentle sobbing sound,
And looking through the gates I saw
A young woman kneeling on the ground.

Her heart was clearly breaking,
she sobbed and cried out with remorse:
"Why did you have to leave me
And go on your heavenly course?"

I couldn't help my sadness,
And so I decided I would cross the lane,
When quite suddenly I got run over,
But I couldn't feel any pain!

My body was laying flat on the ground
And my spirit was floating up in the air,
I was feeling as light as a feather
And I didn't seem to have a care.

I slowly floated over the cemetery
And I could see the young woman there,
Now she was quietly praying
And her eyes were full of despair.

An elderly couple were standing nearby,
And I could tell they were the same as me.
I guessed they were her parents,
It was an awful sad sight to see!

The young woman was crying that she was now all alone
And she had brothers and sisters to keep!
If only she could get herself a job,
Then she'd be able to make ends meet.

Well, I used to own a little company,
That was before I became deceased.
If only I could have given her a job,
It would really have made me pleased.

Then quite suddenly I was whisked away
And found myself at the Pearly Gate,
Saint Peter was there, with his book in his hand,
"C'mon! he cried. "I haven't all day to wait!

Name and place and time of demise?"
So I gave to him the information.
"Oh no, you've come before your time!" he moaned,
"Either that or you've arrived at the wrong station."

And then all of a sudden I was laying back on the road,
And the young woman was leaving the cemetery!
I quickly rushed over and introduced myself,
Then said, "I can offer you work by the plenty!"

"Thank God!" she cried out. "It's a miracle!
I never thought that I would get through the days!"
I gently put my arm around her and said
"God moves in mysterious ways!!"

THE LORD IS OUR GARDENER

My garden is my pride and joy,
I just love to plant and sow,
And when the weather treats it right
It's wonderful how things grow.

But there's a garden much bigger than mine,
And it covers all the earth,
It's tended by our Lord above
Who put all things on this earth.

I can't say that it's his pride and joy,
Because not everything comes up as planned,
Even though the soil is fertile
There's a lot of stones on the land.

To say that he only took six days,
He certainly put in some hours!
And I guess when he decided to add some colour
That's when he gave to us the beauty of flowers.

He created all the elements
With sunshine, thunder and rain!
And gave to his garden four seasons
So that life would always remain!

It's a beautiful thing, is a garden,
But it needs a lot of affection and care,
Maybe that's why the Lord watches over us
To make sure that nature will always be there!

"All things bright and beautiful"
Is a song that I love to recall,
I wonder when God planted out his garden,
If that was the song he liked most of all?

HOME GROWN

I have always wanted a garden,
It's just wonderful watching things grow,
I also like to potter a bit
And select all the seeds that I'll sow.

The weeding's a bit of a bother,
But I accept it as a labour of love,
Mind, some folk grow weeds just like flowers,
They say that they're a gift from above!

Now I get an awful lot of crawling nasties,
And they are a gift just the same,
But I don't let them run rampant,
I squash them - to me they're just fair game!

The weather always appears to be a problem -
Are we going to have enough rain?
I seem to be always hearing the drought call
When water's running away down the drain!

I love to see the garden in the sunshine,
Then I can appreciate what I've put into the soil.
It's just lovely to stand back in admiration
And get pleasure out of the fruit of my toil:

To see young shoots break through into the daylight
Stretching out for the sky up above,
With the sun and the rain showing them favour
And God bathing them in his heavenly love.

It's wonderful to be sat at the table
And to know what you're eating's home grown!
When everyone says how nice it looks,
And it certainly has a taste of its own!!

THE ROSE

I really enjoy sitting in a garden,
Especially in the summertime
When all the flowers are out in bloom
And their perfume is most sublime.

It's strange that not every flower
Gives off a nice scent to your nose,
Some of them smell quite awful
And they don't have the scent of a rose.

Carnations have a lovely aroma
And their colour gives quite a contrast,
When they are cut and put into vases
They're a flower that really does last.

Honeysuckle is one of my favourites,
Its scent really lasts a long time,
And Jasmine has a perfume to savour,
It makes the air smell sweet and fine.

Sweet Pea has a beautiful aroma
And it lingers very gently in the air,
If they are placed in a bowl on the table
Their fragrance really comes out to bare!

Lilac gives off a wonderful perfume,
Just to pass by the blossom is a treat!
It makes your head swim with its fragrance,
And its aroma makes it very hard to beat.

But my favourite of all is the roses!
Each one has a scent of its own,
With their colour and beauty to enchant you
They really are a pride to be grown!

THE ROSE OF ENGLAND

Oh magnificent rose, with your fragrance so rare,
Nothing equals the beauty and elegance you bare!
You gleam in the light of England's esteem
And stand in repose, as though wrapped in a dream.

Oh beautiful flower, I share with you my heart,
To give to my beloved, with my love to impart.
Like you, she holds beauty and a sweet gentle grace
That I know in my heart no other could replace.

An exquisite beauty, man cannot truly portray
On canvas, in stone, or moulded in clay,
With colours so rare, and a wonder of bloom,
It shows off in majesty, and gently shares it's perfume.

When you stand in the garden, head held with demure,
So all can admire you, the rich and the poor,
You hold no distinction, in rank or for place,
You've been put on this earth, so all can share in your grace.

You may wish to meander, or clamber instead,
Or maybe stand alone, or share a whole bed.
Wherever you grow, whatever place you choose,
You bring a beauty to this land, I hope we'll never lose!

You're a blossom of love, with a shape so refined,
A gift sent from heaven, that is truly divine,
Of all of the flowers that I can recall
The rose of England to me is the most precious of all!

IN A COUNTRY GARDEN

In a lovely country garden,
That's where I long to be,
Surrounded with beautiful flowers
And the birds and the bees.

Beneath the shade of a bough
With colourful blossom in bloom,
Only peace and tranquillity
Would be allowed to share my room.

I could laze in contentment
And just while away the hours,
Quietly watching butterflies
On the faces of flowers.

The sweet scent of honeysuckle
Would float in the air,
While sweet peas and nightstock
Their fragrance would bare.

The roses would look sensational
And their petals would sheen,
While lupins and gladioli
Would stand tall to be seen.

The ivy would cling
To the walls, cold and bare,
Adding colour and life
To places with nothing there.

Ladybirds could join me
And share my haven of rest
In their beautiful red
And black spotted vests.

And in the treetops on high
The birds would brightly sing,
Just like angels in the sky
Resting on their wings.

I would see lovely blue sky
With no clouds overhead,
And blissfully repose
With dreams in my head.

In a lovely country garden,
That's where I long to be,
Alone with just my thoughts
And beautiful serenity,

To be at peace with the world
And just blend in with the flowers,
Where blooms shed their fragrance
And minutes last like hours,

In a beautiful country garden
Where loveliness transpires,
That's where my thoughts take me,
Quietly passing away the hours.

I JUST CLOSE MY EYES AND SIGH

One of the most beautiful sounds you will ever hear
Is the wonderful singing of birds,
When you are sat all alone in the garden
They can almost put their songs into words.

It just sounds like a choral competition
For the bird who sings loudest and bright!
I have heard in my time many recordings
But nothing that could equal this might!

It's wonderful to experience this part of nature
And to be accepted as one of the throng,
Just to sit there amidst peace and tranquillity
And listen to the birds' beautiful song.

Why has God given them such lovely voices?
I wish that I could sing half as sweet!
They don't need music, or any prompting,
They just sing to given Mankind a treat!

When I awaken in the morning to their rapture
It gives me a really wonderful start to my day!
It shows that life can have a whole different meaning,
Even if the sky is cloudy or grey.

From treetop to rooftop they warble,
Their trill is so delightful to hear,
I hope they'll be with us forever
Because to me they bring wonderment and cheer!

When I'm sat by myself in the garden
With time slowly drifting by
And I can hear the sweet sound of birds singing,
Then I just close my eyes and sigh!

MISTER SPIDER

Sitting in the garden, with the sun upon my face,
Feeling snug and cosy, in my own special place,
I watched a little spider drop down on a thread
And then proceed to built himself a fine silken web.

How fascinating to watch this insect work away,
From side to side and up and down, he spent no time at play,
He's meticulous in his building and resolute at his task,
There's nothing can deter him, he's building it to last!

He scurries back and forth, and the web begins to grow,
One minute he is running around, the next his pace is slow,
He appears to be trying it out, as he runs around the edge,
And then he darts into the middle, and prods it with his legs.

He has built it from the apple tree, and onto the garden wall,
And when peering through the sunlight, its hardly seen at all,
Now he's scurried into a corner, and he's waiting for his prey,
It's a lovely creation and it's taken most of his day.

Suddenly a slight breeze dislodged a leaf from off the tree,
And it gently brushed the web, as it floated near me,
The spider darted out to see where his meal had landed,
But unfortunate for him, he'll have to go back empty-handed.

A bluebottle has suddenly got caught in his silken web,
He's angrily trying to break away, or soon now he'll be dead!
He's pulling and he's buzzing, and kicking with all his might,
Then out runs mister spider, smiling with delight!

He dashes to the bluebottle, intent on settling his hash,
But the bluebottle's having none of it, and lands him with a bash.
Well, now the spider rushes him, making it a free-for-all,
But the bluebottle suddenly breaks away and buzzes off over the wall!

THE BUTTERFLY

He glides on the wind, like a breath of fresh air,
Then he lands on a leaf, but he wont remain there,
He flits back and forth, like a sunbeam in dance,
I watch in fascination, as he holds me entranced.

Your beauty enthrals me, your shape is so fine,
You waft in the air, like a fine silken twine,
I could paint a picture if you would sit for me there,
But no sooner are you settled than you're up in the air.

Stay near me! I beg him, please don't fly away,
Just stay a little longer, remain motionless, I pray,
Please rest your wings and gently repose on a flower,
Because I could sit watching you, for many an hour.

I follow your antics, as you float through the air,
You have no direction or you don't seem to care,
When you land you're so fragile and delicately light,
I watch you with wonderment, you don't leave my sight.

Suddenly the wind overcomes you and carries you away,
I can see that you're fighting, but he won't let you stay,
Up and over the garden, far away out of sight,
The wind shows no mercy, and howls with delight.

I'm sorry, little butterfly, that you've been taken away,
My garden looks so bare now, I just wanted you to play,
My heart feels so sad that you're no longer here,
And down my cheek I can feel there's a tear.

I DIDN'T STOP AND COMPLAIN!

I was out mushrooming, early one morning,
When I saw a beauty and picked it in the light
And there beneath it - will you believe what I'm saying? -
Were two pixies both having a fight!!

One of them wore a hat that was yellow
And the other wore a hat that was green,
Now the one with the hat that was yellow
Gave the other one the best shiner I've seen.

I picked them up by the scruff of their collars
And I asked them, "What's this all about?"
Then the one with the little yellow hat on
Said, "You keep your flippin' nose out!!"

Now the one with the dirty great shiner
Said, "I'm in love with a beautiful girl!
But this snake in the grass has just told me
That he's been taking her out for a whirl!"

"That isn't nice!" I said to the one in the yellow!
"How would you feel if she was your girl?"
"Oh, she loves me!" he exclaimed, slightly blushing,
"That's the reason I took her out for a whirl!"

"Well, I can see what's wrong with you two fellas,"
I said. "You both want the same girl for your bride!
But fighting isn't the way to settle things,
You have got to let the girl decide!!"

"Come on, you show me the way!" I said quietly,
And gently put them back on the ground.
"Come on then!" said the one in the yellow,
"But she's going to be my bride, I'm bound!"

They led me to a clearing in a corner,
And then they both began calling out,
Then suddenly I was surrounded by pixies!
And they wanted to know, "What's this all about?"

179

I explained to them as briefly as possible
That the two pixies had just had a fight,
And it was all over the love of a lady,
I said to ask her was the only way right!

A beautiful pixie girl walked slowly towards me
And said, "I know what this trouble's about!
But I want nothing to do with those pixies
Because someone else is taking me out!"

"Alright lads!" I said, "You have your answer,
Now shakes hands and forget what's gone on.
There's plenty of pebbles on the shoreline,
Go and pick yourselves a couple, and so long!"

The next morning I walked the same area,
And there they were fighting again!
But now the one in the yellow had the shiner
So this time I didn't stop and complain!

THE TINY ELF

As I was planting in my garden
I saw an elf beneath a leaf!
Suddenly he cried out startled,
"I hope you don't think I'm a thief!"

I looked at him in amazement,
His tights were green, and hat was red,
"I'm usually away before this hour,
But this morning," he stated, "I stayed in bed."

"Are you an elfin?" I asked quietly,
He looked at me, then nodded his head.
"You're not even supposed to see me,"
He chuckled, as he scratched his head.

"Will you bring me luck?" I asked him.
"Could you grant a wish for me?"
"I don't know if I'm lucky!" he stated.
"But I hope you'll leave me be."

"I'm not the best of elves!" he added.
"That's why I'm left on my own.
But I wish I had a wife!" he giggled,
"Then I'd build a proper home."

"If you were to pull yourself together,"
I said, as I shook my head,
"Then maybe you'll find a romance
And then you'll have to get out of bed!"

He looked at me then started crying,
"Tell me!" he begged. "What should I do?
I feel so lonely and despondent
As though my life has fallen through!"

"First you take a bath!" I told him,
"And I'll make your clothes look grand
With a wash and some repairin'

181

Then you won't look so second hand!"

I poured warm water into a bucket
And then he jumped in fully clothed,
Then I handed him some soap and a flannel
And he handed me his dirty clothes.

When he'd finished with his bathing
I handed him his tiny clothes,
He had ruddy cheeks with a fine complexion,
And a tiny red shining nose!

"Thank you, sir, for your attention!"
He smiled, as he got quickly dressed.
I said to him, "There! You look better,
Some lady's going to be impressed."

"I'm sorry I can't grant you wishes!"
He stated, as he walked away,
"But I wish you every happiness
And have good health every day!"

At the same time every morning
I looked for the elf beneath a leaf,
And in my heart I feel a sadness
That he thought I'd made him out a thief.

But then one morning, when the sun was shining,
A tiny couple came to visit me,
Beneath a leaf he introduced her
And they looked as happy as could be.

TWINS??

As I strolled along a riverbank
I saw a pixie holding a fishing rod
"Have you caught many?" I asked him, smiling,
He quietly gave me a nod.

I walked over to where he was sitting,
His bag was full to the brim.
"I didn't know you ate fish!" I stated.
"We eat anything!" he replied with a grin.

I'm going for my lunch now!" he added.
"You are welcome to come along."
"That's very kind of you!" I replied, smiling,
"Home cooking is where I belong."

We both walked away from the river
And walked past a place that I knew
"I've been here before!" I told him.
He said, "I thought that I recognised you!"

"Me and my friend were both fighting
And you made us pack it in!
That's a while ago," he said to me smiling,
"Neither of us really did win!"

We walked along partly through a meadow
And then through a cluster of trees,
Then there gathered around in a circle
Was a ring of pixies, sitting on some leaves.

The largest pixie arose and walked over.
"Welcome!" he said, shaking my hand.
"How nice of you to come and share in our luncheon.
It's fish, and it's going to be grand!"

"I know your face!" he said to me, smiling,
"You're the man who broke up a fight!
Now both of them pixies have got married
And everything has turned out right!"

Now the pixie that I knew had put his hat on
And it was a beautiful, bright-coloured green!
Then another pixie emerged from the circle,
He wore a yellow hat that was nice to be seen!

"Hello!" he said, "It's lovely to see you.
It's a while since I've seen you, my friend!
Now I'd like you to meet my lovely wife,
She's the one who's sitting where the circle ends!"

And then the pixie with the little green hat on
said, "There's my wife, who is close to the end!"
I said, "Just hold on there, you two fellas,
I think I'm going right round the bend!"

They both suddenly burst out laughing
And said, "You told us that neither of us could win!
Then when we met up with our sweethearts
The pair of us married a twin!!"

YOUNG AT HEART

I still keep the flame of youth burning,
It's so sad that I have to grow old,
But the memories of my childhood they linger,
For my past is a happiness to hold.

To remember the joys of my childhood
And the innocence and sweetness of youth,
To share in the simplicity of loving,
And to never doubt the sweet words of truth.

These are things I remember,
The picnics and parties so gay,
The laughter and shouting of children,
As they skipped on the pavement at play.

My mother's embrace as she held me,
With tenderness, and lovingly care,
And my father would tell me tall stories
As I quietly sat in a chair.

Oh, the dreams and aspirations of my childhood,
I hoped they would one day come true,
I wanted to be older and wiser
And do things like grown-up people do.

But now that I'm old and much wiser,
My mind wanders back to the day
When grown-ups had all of the wisdom
And I was just happy to play.

I will always revere with fond memory,
These are things I will never depart,
For this is my one ray of sunshine,
And I will always be young at heart.

MEMORIES

Memories...A compendium of life that's held close to your heart,
Each page is a chapter, each word is a part,
Every memory hold a picture stored away in your mind,
As we've trodden our pathway of good or unkind.

As I turn back the pages of the pathway I've trod,
Maybe the route that I've taken wasn't the right way to God.
But we live our own lives and hope at the end
That the road that we travelled had very few bends.

When in my childhood, my grandparents thought I was blessed,
My mother adored me, my father treated me as a pest.
It's a fifty-fifty start when your father treats you with scorn,
But I've always said to myself, 'I didn't ask to be born!"

I started the nursery, and thought that was pretty good,
The teachers made a fuss of me, and I felt understood.
I moved on to the big school, now that was quite rough,
Because the school that I went to, you had to be tough.

But gaining strength of character, and gaining it in might,
Are two different pathways, for the world you can't fight.
As time moved along, I took on a lovely wife,
But the education from school isn't an education on life.

We started a family, I toiled hard for my pay,
The hours seemed long up till the end of the day.
We had a daughter and two sons: I was proud,
Unlike my father, who didn't want me around.

Now that I'm older and my life has moved on,
I'm left with my memories and I'm glad I was born.
With my loving wife and family and our friends all around,
The pathway I've taken wasn't all stony ground!

WHEN I WAS A BOY

When I was a boy all was a wonderment
And I never saw a cloud in the sky,
The sun seemed to shine forever
And the time simply drifted by.

When I was a boy people liked walking
And took pleasure in hiking afar,
But now all they do is to stand in a queue
And spend their lives parking the car.

When I was a boy people were friendly,
They were happy to meet you and me,
And our doors were always left open
As an invitation of hospitality.

When I was a boy life was deemed precious,
And love was a shared commodity,
I was brought up to respect my elders
And taught to care for the community.

When I was a boy life was simple,
No computers or great technology,
I don't seem to remember pollution
Or great depths of depravity.

When I was a boy people were happy,
But now most appear to be sad,
When you look at the waste and the greed that's in life
That's a good reason to make you feel bad.

When I was a boy life was a wonderment
And I never saw a cloud in the sky,
The sun seemed to shine forever,
But now time is just passing me by.

I'M NEAR THE END OF THE LINE

In our very short childhood days
Life was great then in many ways.
We didn't have any worries, all was just play,
But time passed so quickly, and now I'm turned grey!

We used to often visit the park
And play on the grass, just having a lark,
We never destroyed things, it was all done in fun,
And then we'd charge down the pathway, to see how fast we could run.

It was lovely to see the flowerbeds laid out in display,
And when the sun was out, we would just laze away.
Nobody bothered us, our time was our own
Mind, now and then Mother would have a little moan!

And if we had a ball, then we'd kick it about,
Those were the days, when happiness was shared out.
And if the boating was open, we would go for a row,
Then I would ask, "Please can I have a go?"

I'd see fish in the water, and kids with a net,
And then one would start crying, because he'd got wet,
Then I'd go on the swings, and ask for a push,
Once I slipped off, boy, that ground wasn't half rough!!

And sometimes the band would play in the park,
"That's a nice tune!" I would hear people remark.
I don't remember transistors or ghetto-blasters that roar,
No one went home with ears that were sore!

We had some great times when I was a lad,
There's times I was naughty, but never really bad,
None of us were malicious, we just had a good time,
But now I just feel, I'm near the end of the line.

IT'S BEEN A ROUGH ROAD

My eyes are so tired
That I'm falling asleep,
I am feeling so weary
That I'm dead on my feet.

I need to lay down
And lighten my load,
My legs are like lead
It's been a rough road.

I have seen a lot of trouble
On my pathway through life,
I have seen a lot of torment
Through hardship and strife.

There's a lot of folk need help
Me, I've just battled along,
All that I can offer is
A kind word and a hearty song.

Most folk don't need much
To survive in this life,
Just one or two kids
And the love of a wife.

If the weather treats us fairly,
Well, then it's nice to say
That we hope that tomorrow
Will be another fine day!

Most folk I know are honest
And as straight as a die,
But others need watching
And do nothing but lie.

I just can't see the sense
In people being a thief!
All they bring on themselves
Is a whole lot of grief!

Now, it isn't all that easy
Walking this pathway of life!
There's a lot of folk have fallen
And ended their own life!

What keeps us going?
That's the question I ask!
What gives to us the strength
And the courage to last?

Could it be our beliefs,
Or maybe it's our faith
That carries us forward
And holds us in place?

I can't answer the questions
I've been knocked about and bruised,
Perhaps after I've rested
I'll buy a new pair of shoes!!

AFTER I'M GONE!

After I'm gone, deceased and dead,
I can't see a reason for tears being shed,
I want folk to be happy, they can all sing and dance
I wouldn't mind joining them, given half the chance!!

My mates will all miss me, when I'm no longer here,
I won't be stood at the bar, buying them a beer,
They'll have no one to lean on, when they're stony broke,
And that's when they'll realise that I wasn't a bad bloke!

I have always like people, that's why I've got on,
But most of the old 'uns, have already gone!
I hope I'm remembered as a pretty decent guy,
I've nearly always been honest, and hardly ever told a lie!

If I leave them a will, well what should I say?
"Sorry, the coffers empty, but have a nice day"?
I don't want to hurt folk, maybe if I leave them a token,
But I can't seem to find owt that isn't damaged or broken!

My wife will probably miss me when she's all alone,
She'll have no one to shout at, no one there to moan!
I know that she loves me, I can see it in her eyes,
But after I'm gone, could those eyes have told lies??

I hope I die natural, I want to go in one bit,
I don't want to be like a jigsaw, where no pieces will fit!
Mind, I don't want no pain, just to go in my sleep,
I want to look peaceful, so people won't weep!

Then maybe on my headstone, carved out in bold type,
Would be a few words of what I would like:
Here lies little Thomas Ian, he's gone and got dead,
We hope in the next world, he has a four-poster bed!!

SMELL THE FLOWERS

Please give your life a rest, and smell the flowers,
Our life is short on this earth, please don't burn the hours,
Just relax, take it easy, put your feet up and repose,
Life's just passing us by, and Heaven only knows.

Give yourself some space, and enjoy the time you've got,
Plenty of people have passed this way, some have missed a lot,
You only get one chance at life, so grab it with both hands,
Forget about what you're doing, not all your life needs plans!

Give yourself some time off, and break into the light,
Have a look around you, it doesn't need second sight!
There's a world out there that's living, given to you and me,
So get out there and enjoy it, breathe in some air that's free!

You don't need pots of money, or heaps of untold wealth,
In fact you don't need naught at all to think about your health,
It doesn't need any brain power, and you don't have to sit a test,
Just walk a little slower and give your life the best!

We all tend to get caught up, and let things run away,
It doesn't hurt to put the brakes on, and bring quality into play,
At times it can work wonders, just to stop and think,
Giving yourself a well-earned rest, and halting at the brink.

There's a lot of stress and tension out there on the road,
With an awful lot of people burdened with a load,
It's sad to see their faces, looking weary and worn,
And the misery in their eyes saying, "Why was I ever born?"

So please give your life a rest, and smell the flowers,
Put your feet up off the path of life, and while away some hours.
Take in the light, enjoy the sight and give your life some ease,
Or the only rest that you will get is when you Rest in Peace!!

BELIEVE!

When Man has decided to leave this planet alone
And moved on to bigger things, like another time zone,
Maybe life will return to the places he's binned
And perhaps God will forgive all the times Man has sinned.

When we were born, we brought nothing this way,
And then when we die, we'll take nothing away!
It's just while we're living we offer nothing our respect,
Over half the planet has been treated with neglect.

I don't amount to much, in this world filled with men,
Maybe God will decide to start over again,
And perhaps the mistakes that I think he has made
Won't be repeated, his plans will be better laid.

But life's just a circle, and life still goes on,
I'll get up tomorrow, and hear the birds chirp their song,
The sun will still shine, and the rain will fall down,
There's some people who will smile, while others just frown.

Babies will be born, and people's lives will change,
And lots of events will happen with new things to arrange,
Life's just a ring, it seems to go round and round,
With nature as the core, making everything sound!

I love the seasons that brings life to this land,
I wonder at nature, to me it's so grand,
I respect all nature's life, and I believe in fair play,
And I dream about tomorrow being a whole better day.

I think about our children and hope their lives will be blessed,
That they will never suffer hardship, and never be oppressed,
I hope that their lives are filled with peace and love,
And I hope they believe there's a God up above.

WINTER

The snowflakes float down from the sky up above,
Enveloping the earth like a white woollen glove,
The trees stand majestic in the bleak winter chill,
The only one can hear is of a sweet robin's trill.
The icicles form, from the rooftops on high,
And the winds quickly scatter the clouds across the sky.

The ponds are all frozen, and everything looks bleak,
The swans and the ducks can't stand on their feet,
The children build snowmen, and skate on the ice,
Some fall on their bottoms, and pay a sorely price.
Others throw snowballs and slide down a slope,
And hang on to their sledges, by the means of a rope.

The storm clouds enshroud the light of the day,
And snow comes down thicker on the children at play,
Nothing grows in the garden, not a blade of green,
But watching the children, is such a wonderful scene.
The winds become stronger, and the snow turns to sleet,
Then the kids all rush home, with half-sodden feet.

On hedgerows the holly grows, with its berries of red,
To the wall clings the ivy, with trails hanging like thread,
Most of the animals have hibernated, and are deep in repose,
All snuggled up and warm, out of the winter's icy throes.
Now the snow is much deeper, and the frost is more biting,
So it's time to pull a chair up, to a fire that's inviting.

SPRING

When the sun reaches down, from the heavens above,
And God enshrouds the earth, in the warmth of his love,
A new life in abundance appears from all around,
And tulips and daffodils bring life to the ground,
Blue bells and primroses all join in the throng,
With birds in the treetops, joining them in song.

When the landscape is coated in a carpet of green,
And crocuses and hyacinths appear on the scene,
When azaleas and blossom decide to show their face
And caterpillars become butterflies, full of beauty and grace,
When trees spread their branches and unfold leaves of green
And the beauty of what surrounds us seems almost a dream.

When the newly-born lambs begin to frolic and play,
And the ice and the snow has all melted away,
When the water cascades from the mountains above,
And fills all the rivers, swelling them in flood,
When the land is tilled, and the seeds of corn are sown,
Making for a harvest, when our staff of life is born:

When hedgehogs and porcupines appear in the light,
And the hares and rabbits all play out of sight,
When the days become longer and the dark is less seen,
This wonder of nature makes a miraculous scene.
There has to be a beginning, or we can't have an end,
That's the miracle of nature, it's a God given blend.

SUMMER

When the sky is deep blue, and not a cloud is in sight,
And when the flowers are all blooming, to everyone's delight,
When the sweet smell of honeysuckle and roses fills the air,
And the aroma of sweet pea, their fragrance do bare,
When the landscape's a picture, a beautiful scene,
And the picture's called Summer, framed with God's holy esteem:

When bees collect pollen, that makes honey so sweet,
And we collect strawberries that make a wonderful treat,
When we pick all the damsons, and raspberries galore,
And most of the blackcurrants seem to tumble on the floor,
We make pies and desserts, preserves, crumbles and all,
They complete a wonderful meal, a feast to enthral.

When the Morris men and dancers put on a display,
And we turn out to watch them, and shout our Hurray,
When the bands and parades all march down the street,
And we stand there applauding and stamping our feet,
It's lovely to be there, joining in all the fun,
If only we could have more of this glorious sun.

When the harvest is over, and the bread we all share,
And the fruit from the trees is picked with sweet tender care,
When the children play out, in the warm noon day sun,
And their parents and grandparents join in the fun,
When picnics and rambles are brought to the fore,
That's when this wonderful season is with us once more!

AUTUMN

The nights are drawing in, and the days are less long,
The birds no longer sing their sweet summer song,
The leaves on the trees softly fall to the ground,
Whilst the wind howls in protest, scattering them around.
Petals fall from the flowers, where beauty had been the face,
This is the season of change, at God's given grace.

The days are getting colder, the sun offers us no charm,
We wrap up in our woollies to keep us nice and warm,
The colours change from green, to red, gold and brown,
All over the countryside a fresh picture's etched down.
We see a colourful rainbow that's a halo of love,
Sent down with God's blessing, from the heavens above.

The leaves rustle along the ground, as we shuffle our feet,
It's a whole different sound, as we walk down the street,
The bands are all gone, and the parades are no more,
The children stay inside, they won't stray past the door.
The wind drives the clouds and pushes them out of place,
So that a little rain will fall on everyone's face.

The wind is much colder, and there's a bite in the air,
Now the trees are stood naked with their branches left bare,
The rain pours from the sky, forming puddles all around,
And mist covers the hedgerows until we can't see the ground.
The animals seek shelter, a warm comfortable place,
For their preservation of life and winter's coming embrace!

GOODBYE

Goodbye and farewell, is how we leave you,
Maybe our sentiments should be more,
When we've said our goodbyes forever
And then we turn and walk out through the door.

Goodbye is our final word of parting,
It sounds like we're saying, "It's the end."
It isn't like, "Until we see each other, God bless you!"
Or "We will meet up once again, my friend."

Goodbye seems a sad way of departing,
We wave as our friends fade out of sight.
Our heart holds the sadness of them leaving,
But we hope in the future to unite.

Goodbye, good luck and God bless you,
The sentiments are all there to say,
We don't want the separation to be final,
Because we won't all be together one day.

Goodbye as we hold back the tears,
Farewell as we grip their hands tight,
We will all meet again in the future,
But for me "Goodbye!" just doesn't seem right.

Love and life is how we live
Life is sometimes blue
But love brings out the wonders
That makes us feel brand new!

THE END